creating your chapter harmony

CREATING YOUR
CHAPTER HARMONY

A Guided Journey to Manifest the Life You Deserve

Ryen Watkins

CHAPTER HARMONY PRESS

Sources and permission credits are located on page 269.

Published by Chapter Harmony Press
An imprint of Chapter Harmony LLC
Baltimore, Maryland

For more information, visit chapterharmony.com

Chapter Harmony® is a registered trademark of Chapter Harmony LLC.

ISBN: 979-8-9938331-0-1

Library of Congress Control Number: 2026900479

Edited by Veronica Ojukwu
Book design by Ryen Watkins

Publisher's note: This book is intended for personal growth and reflection. It is not a substitute for medical, mental health, financial, or legal advice. Readers are encouraged to seek professional support as needed.

Printed in the United States of America
First Edition

For my 23-year-old self,
my dream girl.

chapter harmony

\chap-tər här-mə-nē\   noun

---

the state of deciding to align with everything you deserve.

see also: a gentle reminder you deserve to be paid, loved, and rested in high favor.

Welcome to your Chapter Harmony.

This workbook is a 12-month companion, designed to support you in creating a life filled with abundance, pleasure, and romance. You'll find short essays, gentle color therapy, guided prompts, and activities to remind you that everything you need is already within you.

Each chapter offers reflections, songs, affirmations, and inspired quotes to meet you throughout this journey. There is no right or wrong way to move through these pages. Some pages will invite reflection, others will inspire action. Take what aligns, and leave what doesn't.

My hope is that these pages serve as a
gentle reminder:
You are already deserving.
You are already enough.

No matter where you are on your journey,
you can decide to create your Chapter Harmony
today.

You deserve it.

xo, *Ryen*

TABLE OF CONTENTS

Section 3: Sealed in High Favor

"Do you not know that *you* are the temple of God and that
the Spirit of God dwells in you?"— 1 Corinthians 3:16 (NKJV)

Section 1: Opening Ceremony

"Did you know that birds do not land because they're tired?
It is a remembrance.
They know and have always known that their
liberation depends on their ability to recall the ground."
— Cole Arthur Riley, *This Here Flesh* (2022)

NOW PLAYING:
♪ *Feeling Good* — Nina Simone

I, _____, decide to align
with everything I deserve.

Today, I remember who I am.

I am already deserving.
I am already enough.

I welcome my Chapter Harmony, where being paid,
loved, and rested in high favor is my new normal.

I am so excited to see how good it can get.

I deserve it.

_____   _____
SIGNATURE   TODAY'S DATE

PRESS PLAY

First things first, let's set the vibe.
Scan the QR code below for *feels*.

P R E S S   P L A Y

Have you ever heard a song and your whole mood shifts?
You want to dance. You start smiling.
Or sometimes, the gratitude hits so hard it makes you tear up.

The power of music is real.

This playlist was curated to support you as you move
through this book and beyond.

To help you feel good.
To help you stay open.
To help you call in more of what you want:
abundance, romance, pleasure, joy... all of it.

You deserve it.

Now, let the experience *begin*...

MANIFESTATION

The Art of Manifestation

Manifestation is the art of becoming an energetic match to what you desire without forcing or chasing. It's remembering that everything you seek is already seeking you, waiting for your permission to arrive.

> *Everything I seek is already seeking me, waiting for my permission to arrive.*

It starts with **clarity**; getting clear about what you desire. Then expands through **belief**, trusting that it's already on its way. And it is declared through **embodiment**, living as if it's already yours.

You don't need to know the "how." You simply have to hold the frequency of "yes." Instead of asking, "When will this happen for me?" Try, "I'm excited to see how this works out!"

Practicing Manifestation

- Begin with gratitude for what already is.
- Get clear about what you want and how you want to feel.
- Speak it. Write it. Visualize it.
- Feel it in your body. What does it feel like to have it now?
- Surrender the outcome. Let go of control and trust it's on its way to you. *Because it truly is.*

You Are The Magic

"God is not a distant creature, far off in the sweet by and by. God is within you. God lives in you, through you and as you." — Reverend Ike

When you tap into the divine presence within you and become self-aware, you become the co-creator of your life. You are the vessel through which your desires come into form.

You are the magic!
Are you ready to create your Chapter Harmony?

God show me how good it can get!

THE SPACE BETWEEN ASKING *and* RECEIVING

♪ *22:22*, Londrelle

The Art of Surrender

Once you've asked, believed, and embodied. Your next role is to trust.
What do you do while you wait, while you surrender the outcome?
Well, you act like you know.

Patience is the practice of trusting what you can't *yet* see. The space between your prayer and its arrival. The space between asking and receiving.

This is where faith matures.
Where you learn to stay open even when you don't have proof.
Where you remember that your role is to relax, not to worry.

So breathe.
Tend to what's in front of you.
Live like it's already on its way.
Act like you know.

If you're:

Manifesting a **Home**: Care for your current space with love. Clean, declutter, and create beauty where you are.
Manifesting a **Lover**: Get clear about what you want. Are you emotionally, spiritually, and energetically a match to the person you desire? Become what you're praying for.
Manifesting **More Money**: Create places for money to flow. Open the account. Organize your finances. Be ready!
Manifesting **Peace**: Ten minutes of stillness or deep breathing can help you experience calmness within your body right now. Start small.
Manifesting **New Friendships**: Make space for connection. Reach out and nurture the relationships that already feel aligned. Be the friend you want to attract.
Manifesting a **Car**: Research, test drive, and make space in your budget.

Manifesting a **Career Change**: Update your resume or portfolio. Use this time to practice your craft. How can you start showing up as this version of yourself now?
Manifesting **Clarity** or **Purpose**: Follow your curiosity. Ask yourself, "What lights me up?"
Manifesting **Wellness**: Take care of yourself. Rest, hydrate, move your body, and eat foods that make you feel good.
Manifesting **Forgiveness**: Release the grip on the story that hurt you. Be gentle with yourself. When you're ready, try shifting from "Why did this happen to me?" to "What did this teach me? How can I protect myself moving forward?"
Manifesting **Expansion**: Take the first step forward, even if it feels tiny.
Manifesting **Creativity** or **Pleasure**: Make room for play. What inspires you? Music, nature, colors? Be open to how creativity finds you. Do one thing each day that makes you feel good. Reach for laughter when you can.

The following pages are here to help you remember who you are.

You are already deserving.
You are already enough.

NERVOUS SYSTEM

Am I safe?   What if everything falls apart?   This feels too much.

Am I a disappointment?   Am I being misunderstood?

Why am I on edge?   Why can't I relax?   My heart feels heavy.

Is it okay to rest?   I just want to feel at peace.   What else can I fix?

Stop. Pause. Breathe.

Manifestation thrives in safety. When your body feels safe, your energy flows smoothly, your mind relaxes, and your heart becomes open to the goodness waiting for you.

Before you move forward, pause and notice: **How does my nervous system feel right now?**

- What sensations am I feeling in my body right now?
- Do I feel grounded, or am I tense? Am I anxious?
- How's my breath? Shallow, steady, or held?
- Where do I feel openness? Where do I feel tightness?
- What might my body be trying to tell me?

A Regulated Version of Me Feels Like:

- Place one hand over your heart, one on your belly.
- Inhale for a count of four, hold for two, exhale for a count of six.
- Remind yourself: "It's safe to slow down."
- Imagine your breath melting tension away with every exhale.
- Repeat three times, or until your breath feels easier.

5-4-3-2-1 Grounding Technique:

If your body still feels unsettled, try this practice to help ground you in the present moment.

Notice:
- five things you can see
- four things you can feel
- three things you can hear
- two things you can smell
- one thing you can taste

My body is my home.
I return to safety with every breath.

NERVOUS SYSTEM

♫ *In Your Own Home*, Cleo Sol

When I feel overwhelmed, what helps me *return* back to myself?

_____

_____

_____

_____

What does *safety* feel like in my body? (Think sensations, sounds, scents, spaces, people)

_____

_____

_____

_____

If my body had a *voice*, what would it need me to know right now?

_____

_____

_____

_____

I trust my body to guide me home.

self-talk check-in

What do I often say to myself when I make a mistake?

_____

_____

How do I describe myself when no one's listening?

_____

_____

What do I believe others think about me?

_____

_____

How do I respond to compliments or success?

_____

_____

What's one thought I've outgrown, but still return to?

_____

_____

Old Story	New Story
I'm not doing enough.	I'm allowed to move at my own pace.
I'm too emotional.	My emotions are messengers, not weaknesses.
I'm behind.	My timing is divine.
I'm hard to love.	I am love, and I attract it easily.

I speak to myself gently,
with kindness and care.

self-talk check-in

The way you describe yourself shapes the way you move through the world. Remember, your old story is out! Today begins your new story.

Instructions:
- Grab two colored pens or highlighters.
- Circle the words that currently feel true for you already.
- Using a different color, circle the words you're growing into.
- Practice standing in front of the mirror and speaking the words you're growing into aloud. Start with "I AM..."

joyful	expansive	sovereign
grounded	kind	blessed
abundant	courageous	thankful
aligned	forgiving	harmonious
intentional	loving	steady
graceful	balanced	free
magnetic	receptive	rooted
worthy	trusting	brilliant
centered	authentic	divine
evolving	empowered	connected
soft	faithful	magical
strong	nurturing	beautiful
creative	liberated	focused
brave	vibrant	content
wise	groundbreaking	inspired
intuitive	devoted	grateful
patient	compassionate	joyous
confident	adaptable	bold
open	radiant	purposeful
gentle	anchored	energetic
rested	fulfilled	attuned
peaceful	expressive	faith-filled
luminous	curious	secure
disciplined	consistent	playful
resilient	mindful	vulnerable
flowing	whole	healing
self-assured	glowing	gracious

I KNOW WHO I AM

my sacred foundation

 BECAUSE I KNOW ———————————————— WHERE I COME FROM

♫ *As*, Stevie Wonder

Your sacred foundation lives within you, always.
You don't have to know your full story to begin.
You don't need to know every name, every place, or every detail.

This page is an invitation to remember in your own way.

Is there an ancestor whose prayers are the reason you're here? An ancestor whose strength you feel in your spirit, whose presence you sense when you're still? Or, perhaps you carry the energy of someone you've never met?

This can also serve as a space to honor anyone or anything that has helped you become who you are. Not just an ancestor, but an elder, a mentor, a friend, a younger version of yourself, a prayer, a place, or even a memory.

Honor the seen and unseen hands that have guided you here, and all that makes you *you*.

REMEMBRANCE. HONOR. REMEMBRANCE. HONOR. **REMEMBRANCE.** HONOR. REMEMBRANCE.

"And so our mothers and grandmothers have, more often than not anonymously, handed on the creative spark, the seed of the flower they themselves never hoped to see; or like a sealed letter they could not plainly read. Guided by my heritage of a love of beauty and a respect for strength—in search of my mother's garden, I found my own."
— Alice Walker, *In Search of Our Mothers' Gardens* (1983)

I KNOW WHO I AM

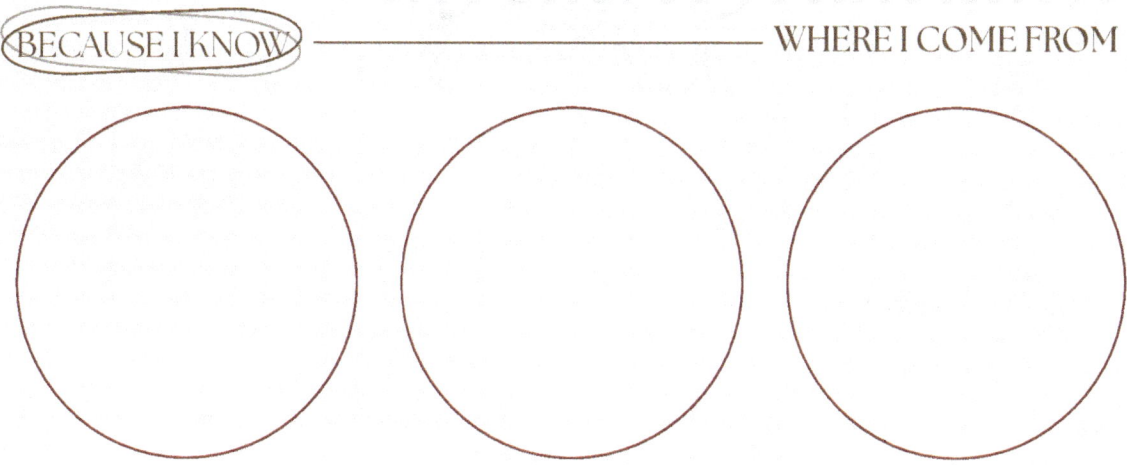

BECAUSE I KNOW ———————————— WHERE I COME FROM

[add a photo or name of the loved one(s) on your mind]

What qualities or gifts have I inherited from these loved ones? What memories or scents come to mind? What do I want to carry forward in their honor? If they could speak to me right now, what message might they be offering me in this moment?

_____
_____
_____
_____
_____
_____
_____
_____
_____
_____
_____
_____
_____

When you feel uncertain or ready to give up, take a deep breath.
Ask yourself: *What would they tell me to do right now?*
What strength or faith would they remind me to reach for?
Let their wisdom move through you. Let them be a gentle
reminder that you are never walking alone.

I am an answered prayer.
Their love lives within me, always.

I AM

I AM

I AM

I AM

ABUNDANT

worthy

falling in love with my life

embodying self love

finding pleasure in my day-to-day

cut & paste
a photo of yourself here

manifesting ease

M

LOVE

AT PEACE

MAGNETIC

loving taking care of myself

I

GRATEFUL

excited for what's to come!

healthy & happy

I AM

VISION BOARD

My Word or Theme for this year:
(examples: Ease, Romance, Overflow, Abundance, Expansion)

_____

This year, I want to feel...
(describe the emotions you want to experience daily)

_____
_____
_____
_____
_____

This year, I am a woman who...	How will I protect my peace, nourish my body, and honor my rest?

What are my money goals, business goals, or passions that deserve energy this year?	How do I want to be loved? By myself and by others?

DAILY AFFIRMATIONS

MONEY FLOWS TO ME IN OVERFLOW.

I AM OPEN TO RECEIVING MORE. THIS IS EASY.

MONEY AND MAGIC MEET ME WHEREVER I GO.

I AM MAGNETIC TO LOVE AND MEANINGFUL CONNECTIONS.

I AM DEEPLY LOVED AND WORTHY EXACTLY AS I AM.

I AM SURROUNDED BY LOVE THAT FEELS WARM AND SAFE.

I CHOOSE REST WITH EASE.

I HONOR MY BODY'S SIGNALS. IT IS SAFE TO SLOW DOWN.

I AM WORTHY OF REST THAT TRULY RESTORES ME.

100 SOLO DATES *Activity Bucket List*

♫ *Private Party*, India.Arie

Romanticizing Everyday Life

- Spend the day with your *Creating Your Chapter Harmony* Workbook
- Create a vision board (see page 16)
- Discover your signature scent
- Redecorate a room or cozy corner in your home
- Buy yourself flowers, and add a handwritten love note to yourself
- Cook your favorite meal
- Watch your favorite childhood movie
- Watch the sunrise
- Watch the sunset
- Start a gratitude jar (see page 235)
- Have a self-care pampering day with DIY facials
- Send flowers to a friend or family member
- Have a solo picnic in the park
- Take yourself on a digital detox day
- Light candles, play your favorite music, and take a goddess bath (see page 54)
- Plan a staycation at a nearby hotel
- Build a blanket fort and read a book inside
- Go to a movie and bring your favorite candy
- Buy a piece of jewelry that symbolizes your growth
- Dance to your favorite album
- Reorganize or declutter a space in your home
- Take yourself to brunch and turn your phone off
- Buy something cozy: a new robe, pajamas, blanket, pillow, etc.
- Treat yourself to something new, big or small
- Order takeout from your favorite restaurant and start a new television series
- Rest in bed with your favorite book and beverage
- Visit a spa and treat yourself to a massage

Learning & Growth

- Volunteer for a cause that moves you
- Visit a bookstore and buy a book that feels meant for you
- Learn a simple song on an instrument
- Listen to a new podcast or audiobook about a topic that sparks your curiosity
- Learn a new language (start by downloading a free app like Duolingo)
- Watch a documentary that expands your perspective

Creativity & *Expression*

- Try a dance class
- Take a pottery or painting class
- Try a DIY craft
- Cook a new international dish
- Experiment with a new hairstyle or makeup look
- Try crocheting
- Explore a new fragrance
- Paint your nails a color that makes you feel powerful
- Try a new baking recipe (see page 265)
- Take a cooking class
- Attend a poetry or open mic night
- Create a photo shoot of yourself (your phone and a tripod will do!)
- Write a poem about how you want to feel this year
- Make a collage from old magazines
- Visit a craft store, browse the aisles, and find an activity that speaks to you
- Do a color analysis test
- Try coffee or tea tasting
- Cook a meal that you loved as a child
- Discover your love language and plan a solo day to honor it
- Bake something to share with friends, neighbors, or coworkers
- Try a sound bath or guided meditation
- Spend the afternoon completing a puzzle
- Print and frame a photo of yourself

Inspiring *Reflection*

- Journal three things you're grateful for before bed
- Write ten things you've forgiven yourself for, then safely burn the paper
- Write a list of things that make you feel safe
- Have an intentional slow morning without your phone
- Write about something or someone that inspires you
- Write a thank-you letter to the version of yourself who kept going, even when it was hard
- Record a voice note to your future self
- Go stargazing and make a wish
- Sit by the water and journal about how you're feeling
- Reflect on an age or version of yourself that needed more love and attention. Look through old photos and write a heartfelt letter. Remind yourself that you are safe, loved, and worthy.
- Reconnect with a hobby you loved as a child
- Revisit an old journal and reflect on how much you've grown
- Sit under a full moon and set a new intention
- Make a list of what abundance looks like to you
- Describe your dream day, from start to finish, as if it already happened (see page 177)
- Write ten things that make you feel luxurious
- Write a love letter to your body (see page 137)
- Write a list of things you've accomplished this year
- Try mirror gazing, look at yourself, and recite affirmations (see page 12)

Adventure & Exploration

- Visit a museum or art gallery
- Explore a new neighborhood or nearby town
- Go wine tasting
- Be a tourist in your own city
- Go on a color therapy walk, choose a color, then look for it in your surroundings
- Plan a solo day trip to the beach
- Take a scenic drive with your favorite playlist
- Visit a botanical garden
- Visit a farmer's market
- Take a train ride
- Go on a hike or long walk and journal at the top/end
- Go to a concert
- Attend a local festival
- Go ice or roller skating
- Spend the day at an art fair or thrift store
- Go to a café and people watch
- Visit your local library
- Go for a scenic bike ride
- Dress up and take yourself to dinner
- Practice yoga or stretching with intention
- Purchase a new plant and commit to caring for it
- Spend the day at the zoo
- Try a new fitness class
- Take a short road trip and try a new restaurant or café
- Visit a planetarium or aquarium

CYCLE HARMONY

♫ *Orange Moon*, Erykah Badu

Just as nature moves through seasons and phases, our bodies carry a *similar* flow, reminding us to pause, to create, to celebrate, and to rest. The same God who set the moon in motion and created each season with intention, created our bodies with intention and wisdom as well.

Let's explore how the menstrual cycle mirrors the moon's phases and the seasons, offering a map to move *with* our bodies instead of against them.

*If your cycle is irregular, or if you don't have a menstrual cycle at all, you can still align with nature's rhythm as a guide.

Menstrual (New Moon)

(Day 1-5)

RELEASE

Your inner winter. A time to slow down, reset, and release what no longer aligns. Honor rest and set intentions for this new cycle.

Movement: stretching, yoga, or walking.

Nutrition: Warm, grounding meals. Iron-rich, omega-3s, and anti-inflammatory foods.

Follicular (Waxing Moon)

(Day 6-13)

CREATE

Your inner spring. Fresh energy blooms and creativity flows. Tap in! This is the perfect time to brainstorm, explore new ideas, and follow what excites you!

Movement: pilates, light cardio.

Nutrition: Lean proteins, healthy fats, complex carbs, and fiber.

Ovulation (Full Moon)

(Day 14)

EXPAND

Your inner summer. You're magnetic, social, and radiant. Let yourself expand. Connect, share, celebrate, and be seen!

Movement: dance, group fitness, HIIT, or other high-energy workouts.

Nutrition: Lean proteins, healthy fats, complex carbs, leafy greens and hydrating veggies.

Luteal (Waning Moon)

(Day 15-28)

REFLECT

Your inner autumn. A time to ground and prepare for stillness. Reflect and refine what needs adjusting. What feels out of alignment? What needs your attention?

Movement: gentle strength training, walking, or yoga.

Nutrition: Complex carbs, anti-inflammatory foods, and healthy fats. Magnesium-rich snacks (bananas, dark chocolate, or nuts).

Remember: The moon's phases shift every month and won't fall on the same dates, just like the menstrual cycle. Use a menstrual tracker or moon calendar each month to check the dates of each phase before aligning.

DAYS OF THE WEEK

ALLOW THE ENERGY OF THE WEEK TO GUIDE YOU ————

Just like you, everything was created with intention. What day of the week were you born? Which day's energy do you naturally align with most? Which one do you resist? What might it be trying to teach you? Try moving with the energy of each day and see how it feels.

MONDAY -- MOON DAY

ENERGY: REFLECTION, EMOTION, INTUITION, REST

IDEAS: JOURNAL, SET GENTLE INTENTIONS, NOURISH YOURSELF WITH COMFORT FOODS, MOVE SLOWLY

> I ENTER TODAY REFRESHED AND RENEWED. I ALLOW MY EMOTIONS TO MOVE FREELY THROUGH MY BODY. I HONOR MY FLOW.

TUESDAY – MARS DAY

ENERGY: COURAGE, MOVEMENT, ACTION, CONFIDENCE

IDEAS: TACKLE CHALLENGING TASKS, DO A STRONG WORKOUT, SPEAK YOUR TRUTH, INITIATE SOMETHING NEW

> I'M EXCITED TO STAND UP FOR MYSELF AND HONOR MY STRENGTHS. I RADIATE CONFIDENCE AND COURAGE IN ALL THAT I FACE TODAY.

WEDNESDAY – MERCURY DAY

ENERGY: COMMUNICATION, CREATIVITY, CLARITY, CONNECTION

IDEAS: PLAN YOUR WEEK, WRITE, REACH OUT TO A FRIEND, BRAINSTORM & CREATE

> I AM IN TUNE WITH ALL PARTS OF ME. I ENJOY COMMUNICATING AND EXPRESSING MYSELF TO OTHERS. I'M EXCITED TO SEEK CLARITY IN EVERY WAY.

THURSDAY – JUPITER DAY

ENERGY: ABUNDANCE, EXPANSION, WISDOM, GRATITUDE

IDEAS: PRACTICE GRATITUDE, STUDY OR LEARN SOMETHING NEW, MAKE BUSINESS OR FINANCIAL MOVES, EXPRESS GENEROSITY

> TODAY I EXPAND MY MIND AND MYSELF WITH PURPOSE AND GRACE. I AM A LIMITLESS BEING OF POSITIVE EXPANSION. MY POSSIBILITIES ARE ENDLESS.

FRIDAY – VENUS DAY

ENERGY: LOVE, BEAUTY, PLEASURE, ART, RELATIONSHIPS

IDEAS: PAMPER YOURSELF, CREATE ART, GO ON A DATE, CONNECT WITH LOVED ONES

> I AM THE EMBODIMENT OF DIVINE LOVE, BEAUTY, AND PLEASURE. I DESERVE LOVE IN HIGH FAVOR.

SATURDAY – SATURN DAY

ENERGY: GROUNDING, BOUNDARIES, DISCIPLINE, REFLECTION

IDEAS: TEND TO RESPONSIBILITIES, RUN ERRANDS, ORGANIZE, REVIEW YOUR GOALS, BE INTENTIONAL

> I HONOR MY BOUNDARIES AND MY INTUITION. I MAKE TIME TO CREATE A PLAN TO ACHIEVE MY GOALS. I ENJOY MY RESPONSIBILITY AS THE CO-CREATOR OF MY LIFE.

SUNDAY – SUN DAY

ENERGY: RENEWAL, CLARITY, CONNECTION

IDEAS: SPEND TIME IN STILLNESS, ATTEND CHURCH OR LISTEN TO AN UPLIFTING MESSAGE, CELEBRATE YOURSELF

> I HONOR MY PROGRESS, MY SUCCESS AND MY FLOW. TODAY I EASILY AND EFFORTLESSLY RELAX, RECHARGE, AND TAKE CARE OF MYSELF.

CHAKRA HEALING

BALANCING YOUR ENERGY CENTERS

THE CROWN CHAKRA SAYS, "I KNOW"

Do you feel spiritually connected?
If not, try: quiet meditation, breathwork, prayer, or yoga.

I AM THE EMBODIMENT OF DIVINITY AND PEACE. I AM WHOLE.

THE THIRD EYE CHAKRA SAYS, "I SEE"

Do you trust your intuition? If not, try: paying attention to the signs & patterns around you, practicing presence, or limiting screen time/distractions.

I AM INTUITIVE, WISE, AND OPEN. I TRUST THE DIVINE TIMING OF MY LIFE.

THE THROAT CHAKRA SAYS, "I EXPRESS"

Do you express yourself with ease? If not, try: speaking your truth out loud, journaling freely, practicing active listening, or singing to release your voice.

I EXPRESS MYSELF WITH CONFIDENCE, LOVE, AND HONESTY. I SPEAK WITH EASE.

THE HEART CHAKRA SAYS, "I LOVE"

Do you feel open to love and connection? If not, try: practicing gratitude and forgiveness, reflecting on your relationships, or volunteering your time to others in need.

I GIVE AND RECEIVE LOVE EFFORTLESSLY & UNCONDITIONALLY. MY HEART SPACE IS OPEN.

THE SOLAR PLEXUS CHAKRA SAYS, "I CAN"

Do you feel clear and confident? If not, try: spending time in the sun, taking inspired action toward what excites you, or speaking words of encouragement to yourself.

I RADIATE CONFIDENCE, LIGHT, AND PEACE. I HONOR MYSELF IN ALL WAYS.

THE SACRAL CHAKRA SAYS, "I FEEL"

Do you feel out of balance creatively, sexually, or emotionally? If so, try: dancing or moving your body, expressing yourself through art, or releasing what no longer nourishes you.

I FLOW WITH THE RHYTHM OF LIFE. I EMBRACE CREATIVITY, PLEASURE, AND SENSUALITY.

THE ROOT CHAKRA SAYS, "I AM"

Do you feel safe, grounded, and supported? If not, try: connecting with nature, decluttering your space, or engaging in physical exercise.

I AM SAFE, PROTECTED, AND SECURE. ABUNDANCE IS MY BIRTHRIGHT.

REACH FOR A — HIGHER FREQUENCY

EMOTIONAL FREQUENCY

Take a moment to check-in with yourself. Where are you on the emotional frequency chart? Wherever you are is okay. No judgment. When you're ready, how can you reach for a slightly *higher* frequency? What would feel supportive: a deep breath, a moment of gratitude, a song, or even a person you can reach for?

what's my *next* thought?

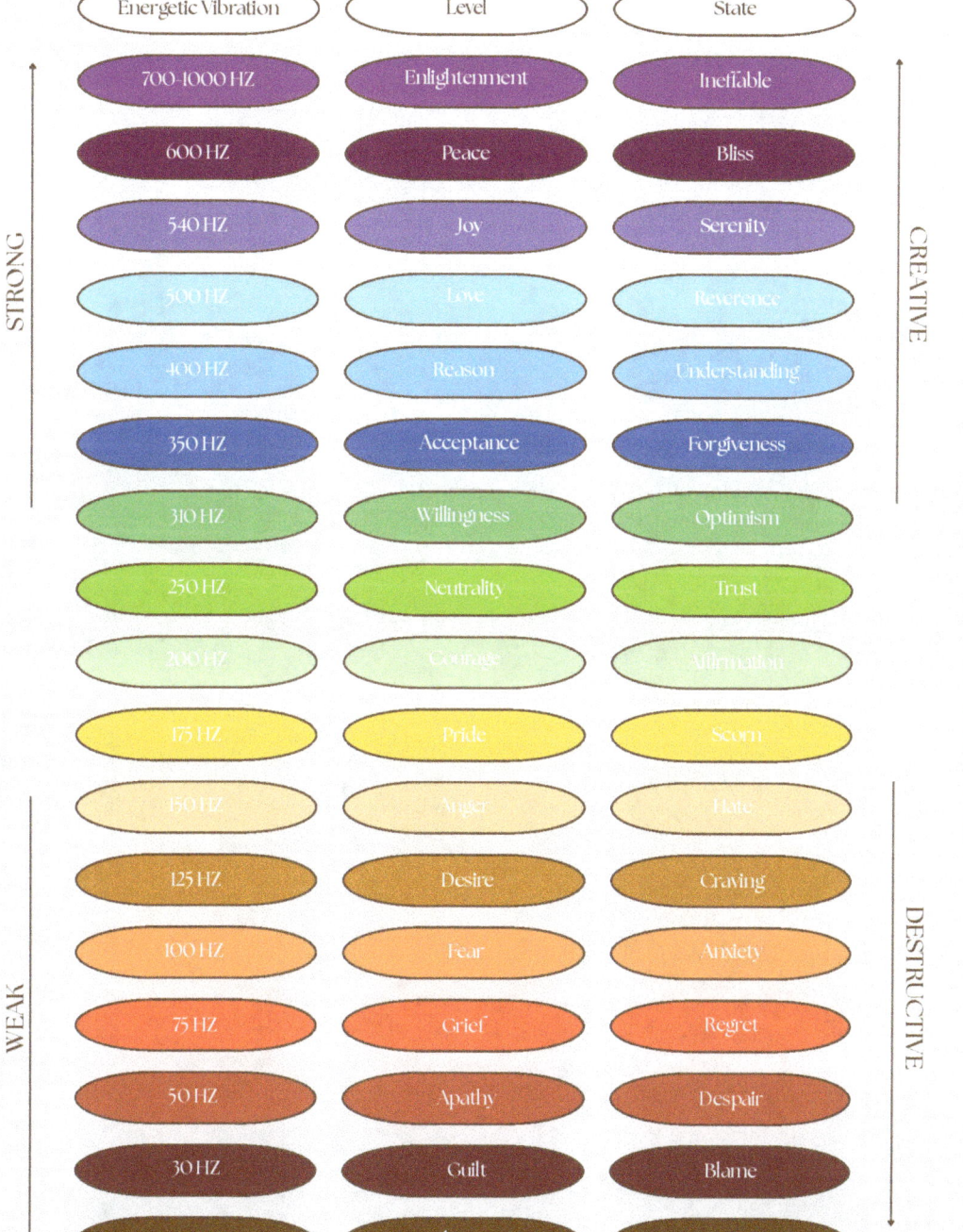

Energetic Vibration	Level	State
700-1000 HZ	Enlightenment	Ineffable
600 HZ	Peace	Bliss
540 HZ	Joy	Serenity
500 HZ	Love	Reverence
400 HZ	Reason	Understanding
350 HZ	Acceptance	Forgiveness
310 HZ	Willingness	Optimism
250 HZ	Neutrality	Trust
200 HZ	Courage	Affirmation
175 HZ	Pride	Scorn
150 HZ	Anger	Hate
125 HZ	Desire	Craving
100 HZ	Fear	Anxiety
75 HZ	Grief	Regret
50 HZ	Apathy	Despair
30 HZ	Guilt	Blame
1-20 HZ	Shame	Humiliation

STRONG · WEAK

CREATIVE · DESTRUCTIVE

I'm *excited* to figure this out

how can I move from resistance to *relief?*

Section 2: Guided Journey

MONTH ONE:
REST
AND
RESET

"Caring for myself is not self-indulgence;
it is self-preservation,
and that is an act of political warfare."
— Audre Lorde, *A Burst of Light* (1988)

chapter one.

June 28, 2023

*Y*ou keep pushing, keep doing, keep proving, though everything in you is saying *enough*.

Rest.

I used to think rest was something to be earned. Even when my body signaled that I had done enough to finally slow down, I told myself I couldn't afford it. I'm so sorry, poor body of mine, but we must keep going!

'Til the wheels fall off, right?

But what if rest isn't something we earn, but instead something we **need**? What if rest is more than a midday nap or eight hours of sleep? What if rest is our gentle reminder that we are not a machine, a reminder that we deserve to feel safe and at ease within our bodies?

In 2021, I was working a job that, on paper, checked every box: great pay, unlimited PTO, and the comfort of working from home. It should have felt easy. It should have felt safe.

But instead, it felt like my spirit was shrinking.

I didn't feel seen.
I didn't feel heard.

No matter how many times I tried to convince myself to keep pushing through: *Girl, this is easy. You're fine. Everyone's tired.* It felt like each day my world became smaller and smaller.

I was exhausted from overextending myself. I was exhausted from pretending. I was exhausted in a way no nap could fix.

Sundays were scary. Like clockwork, my chest would tighten from anxiety around 3 p.m. I was recharging just enough to survive another week.

One day during a review, my manager told me, "You're the calmest person I've ever met." And that line stuck with me. If I am giving this job the calmest version of me while feeling like I was falling apart inside... what would it look like to give that calm back to myself? Didn't I deserve that same calm in return?

Reset.

From that moment forward, I knew something had to change. Yes, I work here, but this is not my whole life.

I knew I needed to start setting boundaries.
So when I logged off, I logged off.

That meant deleting Slack from my phone, muting the

11 p.m. and 6 a.m. texts that used to jolt me awake. At first, it felt uncomfortable, like I was breaking an unspoken rule.

What if they needed me?
Well, *I needed me too.*

I didn't have the capacity to give them *all* of me anymore. I asked myself: *How can I prioritize feeling at ease before entering the chaos?*

I started showing up intentionally during my morning routine. 6 a.m. to 9 a.m. was for me.
I moved my body. Ate breakfast.

I began being intentional throughout the day as well. I took breaks without apologizing. Ate lunch at my kitchen table instead of my desk.

Then it was time to honor my body's need for a new environment.

I started researching new opportunities. What new skills could I learn? What certifications could I pursue? If this wasn't where I wanted to be, then what was?

And slowly, I started to feel in control again.

Sometimes a reset feels less like a breakthrough and more like a deep breath. Sometimes it's not a major life change, but a series of little devotions that say, *I choose me.*

NOW PLAYING:
♪ *Exhale (Shoop Shoop)* — Whitney Houston

REST AND RESET

Where have I been overextending or pushing past my limits?
When was the last time I felt safe doing *nothing*? Where in my life do I
crave softness, even if I don't know how to receive it yet? How can I give
myself permission to pause without needing to prove anything?

_____
_____
_____
_____
_____
_____
_____
_____
_____
_____
_____
_____
_____
_____
_____
_____
_____
_____
_____
_____
_____
_____
_____
_____

REST IS NOT A REWARD; IT IS WHERE I BEGIN. I NO LONGER CHASE EXHAUSTION. I CHOOSE REST AS MY FOUNDATION.

Note four days this month when you intentionally chose to rest and reset. What did you do (or not do) that allowed you to rest? Was it saying "no" when you'd usually say "yes"? Lying in bed for an extra hour? How did it make you feel? What did you learn by giving yourself permission to slow down? Was this difficult for you in any way?

Date:

What did rest look like today?

How did I feel before and after?

What did I learn from this moment?

Date:

What did rest look like today?

How did I feel before and after?

What did I learn from this moment?

Note four days this month when you intentionally chose to rest and reset. What did you do (or not do) that allowed you to rest? Was it saying "no" when you'd usually say "yes"? Lying in bed for an extra hour? How did it make you feel? What did you learn by giving yourself permission to slow down? Was this difficult for you in any way?

Date:

What did rest look like today?

How did I feel before and after?

What did I learn from this moment?

Date:

What did rest look like today?

How did I feel before and after?

What did I learn from this moment?

○ New Moon (Menstrual)	Release.
◑ Waxing (Follicular)	Create.
● Full Moon (Ovulation)	Expand.
◐ Waning (Luteal)	Reflect.

Notice when your body naturally asked for rest this month. Were there moments when your pace slowed without you planning it? What did your body or mood teach you about your natural flow?

Menstrual (New Moon)
R E L E A S E

Follicular (Waxing Moon)
C R E A T E

Ovulation (Full Moon)
E X P A N D

Luteal (Waning Moon)
R E F L E C T

If your cycle is irregular, or if you don't have a menstrual cycle at all, try aligning with the moon as a guide. *Remember:* The moon's phases shift every month and won't fall on the same dates, just like the menstrual cycle. Use a menstrual tracker or moon calendar each month to check the dates of each phase before aligning.

REST AND RESET

INCOME	AMOUNT
TOTAL:	

DEBT	PROGRESS
TOTAL:	

FIXED EXPENSES	ESTIMATE	SPENT
TOTAL:		

VARIABLE EXPENSES	ESTIMATE	SPENT
TOTAL:		

SAVINGS INTENTION	ACTUAL
TOTAL:	

UNEXPECTED BLESSINGS	AMOUNT
TOTAL:	

Let's reset. Where is my money going? What expenses, subscriptions, or habits no longer align?

_____

_____

_____

_____

Take a deep breath, relax your shoulders, and notice how abundance showed up for you this month. No judgment. Think of this page as a money journal, not a budget. If this feels overwhelming at any point, pause, take a break, and return when you're ready. *Remember*: awareness is progress.

gentle reminder

Listen to yourself.
You are allowed to pause.
You deserve to feel safe
and at ease within your body.
Rest is productive.
Rest does not need to be earned.
Your body will speak in
whispers before it shouts.
The world will wait while
you return to yourself.

MONTH TWO:
LOVE AND SOFTNESS

"I have the nerve to walk my own way,
however hard, in my search for reality,
rather than climb upon the rattling wagon of wishful illusions."
— Zora Neale Hurston, from a letter to Countee Cullen (1943)

chapter two.

January 2, 2021

I've always been a lover girl.

The year was 1997. I was curled up on the couch watching Rodgers & Hammerstein's *Cinderella* with Brandy and Whitney Houston. I don't know if it was seeing a Black woman portrayed as a princess for the first time, but my whole body leaned in. Heart wide open. Eyes glued to the screen, mesmerized by the music, the magic, the fairytale. I saw myself, and I knew I wanted to be swept off my feet.

When Halloween rolled around, there was never a question. "Ry, who do you want to be this year?" Cinderella. Always, Cinderella.

I believed in big, cinematic, magical love; the kind that finds you across a crowded room. The love-at-first-sight, I've met you before, kind of love. I'd rewatch *Coming to America* over and over, mesmerized by how the Black girl next door became royalty in the blink of an eye. In my daydreams, my prince was somewhere out there plotting how he'd find me. Would it be in the middle of New York City? Would he come from across the country? Across the world?

Love felt like a destiny.
I couldn't wait to get there, to feel that. To be chosen.

Being chosen, to me, was proof that you were special.
I wanted that proof.

Love would make you new.
Love would make you whole.
Love would grant you a happily-ever-after.

And maybe little me, the girl who believed so deeply in
fairytales (and still does), just wanted to be seen, to be
chosen, to be found.

Maybe she just wanted to be enough.

But as I grew older, the kind of love I found myself in
felt nothing like the love I'd dreamed about in my living
room. Surely this couldn't be what my princess friends
were feeling?

This wasn't the magic I thought it would be.
This *hurts*.

Why am I being treated this way? Why am I forcing
someone to see me?

I thought love would be enough.
This is hard.

The butterflies I once imagined turned into anxiety.
The fairytales I loved so much never prepared me for

the kind of love that left me questioning myself. Each relationship pulled me further from that wide-eyed little girl who believed that love was supposed to make you shine, not shrink.

I started mistaking effort for love, believing that if I worked hard enough, sacrificed enough, proved enough, maybe *this* would finally be it. Maybe this time I'd be chosen, and it would all feel like the movies again.

But instead, I felt smaller. Duller.
I didn't sign up for this.
I signed up for magic.

Then one day, I stopped.
I stopped chasing the kind of love that required me to disappear. I stopped waiting to be seen. I stopped waiting to be found. I decided, rather than making small talk with men just because I was bored, why not get to know, get to like, and get to love myself a little deeper?

For the last twelve months, that's exactly what I did. I chose to be intentionally single.

A year of not waiting or hiding. Just a year dedicated to learning myself and my interests.

Any time I felt lonely or was tempted to call someone who no longer served me, I'd go and do something for myself instead. I took a walk, I called a friend, I tried a new baking recipe. The more I listened to myself, the more natural it became. What makes me feel safe? What feels like love in my body? How can I meet my own needs today?

I started therapy and learned that I am lovable while still learning, while still healing, while still growing.

On May 9, 2020, I hosted my first virtual event. I remember the feeling coming up, "I want to share this with someone." So instantly, I opened my journal and wrote the words I wanted to hear. *Ryen, you did it! I am so proud of you. Your event was amazing. You are a star. Keep going, my love.*

In that moment, I knew self-love was my healing.

I am whole, without the noise of partnership.
My worth does not need a witness to exist.
Love is not labor.
Love is listening.
Love is how I speak to my reflection.
Love is how I pour my tea.
Love is pushing back the curtains and taking a deep breath as the sunlight touches my face in the morning.
Love is patient.
Love is kind.

I am love.

NOW PLAYING:
♪ *Find Someone Like You* — Snoh Aalegra

LOVE AND SOFTNESS

What small acts make me feel seen or desired? How can I mirror those small acts back to myself? What does my body crave when it's asking for love? How can I speak to myself like someone I love deeply?

_____
_____
_____
_____
_____
_____
_____
_____
_____
_____
_____
_____
_____
_____
_____
_____
_____
_____
_____
_____
_____
_____

GODDESS BATH

FOR CLEANSING, RELEASING, AND RECEIVING

WHAT YOU'LL NEED:

- **Time:** Dedicate time to cleansing, releasing, and receiving.
- **Salt:** Choose a bath salt, such as Epsom or Himalayan.
- **Oils:** Choose nourishing oils: coconut, olive, castor, or essential oils; whatever you like!
- **Herbs or Flowers:** Add in whatever calls you; rose petals for love, chamomile for relaxation, lavender for calmness, etc.
- **Light:** Light a candle or dim the lights to create your ambiance.
- **Sound:** Play music that feels good and relaxing, or bathe in silence.
- **Fragrance:** Mist your bath with your favorite perfume or scent.

HOW TO BEGIN:

- **Set your intentions:** What do I want to release? What do I want to receive?

- **Prepare the water:** Run your bath to a temperature that feels comforting and inviting.

- **Create your bath experience:** Add your salts, oils, and herbs. Light your candles. Press play on your music. Spray your fragrance.

- **Enter and enjoy** the experience you've created for yourself.

- **As you soak,** remind yourself of the intentions you've set.

I soften into love,
again and again.

THE WAY I LOVE MYSELF SETS THE TONE FOR HOW THE WORLD LOVES ME.

Take note of four ways you expressed love to yourself this month.
Physically, emotionally, spiritually, financially, and creatively.

Date:

What did I do to show myself love?

How did it make me feel?

What did this moment teach me about
what love looks like to me?

Date:

What did I do to show myself love?

How did it make me feel?

What did this moment teach me about
what love looks like to me?

Take note of four ways you expressed love to yourself this month.
Physically, emotionally, spiritually, financially, and creatively.

Date:

What did I do to show myself love?

How did it make me feel?

What did this moment teach me about
what love looks like to me?

Date:

What did I do to show myself love?

How did it make me feel?

What did this moment teach me about
what love looks like to me?

○ New Moon (Menstrual)   Release.
◑ Waxing (Follicular)   Create.
● Full Moon (Ovulation)   Expand.
◐ Waning (Luteal)   Reflect.

Notice when you felt most open or expressive this month. What moments invited you to reach for love and care? From others, from yourself? Were there phases where love felt easier to give or harder to receive?

Menstrual (New Moon)	*Follicular* (Waxing Moon)
R E L E A S E	C R E A T E

Ovulation (Full Moon)	*Luteal* (Waning Moon)
E X P A N D	R E F L E C T

If your cycle is irregular, or if you don't have a menstrual cycle at all, try aligning with the moon as a guide. *Remember*: The moon's phases shift every month and won't fall on the same dates, just like the menstrual cycle. Use a menstrual tracker or moon calendar each month to check the dates of each phase before aligning.

INCOME	AMOUNT
TOTAL:	

DEBT	PROGRESS
TOTAL:	

FIXED EXPENSES	ESTIMATE	SPENT
TOTAL:		

VARIABLE EXPENSES	ESTIMATE	SPENT
TOTAL:		

SAVINGS INTENTION	ACTUAL
TOTAL:	

UNEXPECTED BLESSINGS	AMOUNT
TOTAL:	

How can I spend in ways that feel loving, not lack-filled or impulsive? What purchase would truly nourish me this month?

_____

_____

_____

_____

Take a deep breath, relax your shoulders, and notice how abundance showed up for you this month. No judgment. Think of this page as a money journal, not a budget. If this feels overwhelming at any point, pause, take a break, and return when you're ready. *Remember*: awareness is progress.

gentle reminder

You deserve the same
gentleness you offer others.
You do not need to
shrink to be chosen.
You are already the magic.
Love is patient.
Love is kind.
You are love.

MONTH THREE:
MONEY AND MAGNETISM

"All successful life is adaptable, opportunistic, tenacious, interconnected, and fecund. Understand this. Use it. Shape God."
— Octavia E. Butler, *Parable of the Sower* (1993)

chapter three.
March 8, 2021

*P*icture me in my kitchen, "This Is for the Lover in You" by Shalamar playing softly in the background. I'm dancing barefoot between the counter and the oven, finding immense joy in experimenting with new ways to decorate. *How can I make it pretty? What else can I add?*

What started as a hobby quickly became sacred. Baking and decorating cakes turned into my version of love notes.

By July 2020, I'd perfected my pineapple upside-down cake. My first thought was that my mom and my grandparents have to try this. I wrapped some up and took it over to them, smiling from ear to ear. Their faces lit up. The joy of sharing my cakes, of watching them savor their first bite. It. Filled. Me. Right. Up.

Soon, I started posting my cakes on social media. Then, people began to notice. I wasn't thinking about profit, pricing, or potential. I was just having fun.
"Ry, do you sell these?" "How much for one?" "I need another one of your cakes!"

God rewards us for listening to ourselves. For following

our light. For doing the things that make us feel alive, not because they make sense, but because they make us *us*.

I laughed every time someone asked. Me? Sell cakes? I was just in here playing around, following the spark.

When I finally did say yes to orders, I lowballed myself completely. "Oh, just give me whatever," I'd say. Comparing cake prices at the supermarket, $20 is fine.

At first, the joy carried me.
But slowly, exhaustion crept in; the kind that comes from pouring without receiving enough back.
My love offering had turned into labor.

The same cakes that once filled my kitchen with sweetness began to taste like fatigue.
That's when I realized something I'll never forget:
When you underprice your gifts, you also undervalue your energy. And when you undervalue your energy, even the things that once brought you joy begin to drain you.

I liked the idea of getting paid to have fun, but what if people thought my prices were too high? What if they decided to just buy a cake from Costco and keep moving?

It was the same belief I'd carried for years, that to deserve anything good, I had to overextend. That exhaustion somehow equaled excellence.

She's tired, she's up all night, she must be successful, she must be doing something right!
Maybe she is, or maybe she's just tired.

It took me a while to realize that undercharging wasn't just about money; it was about identity. *I'll make myself smaller so you feel comfortable paying me.*

Scarcity lives in more than our wallets; it lives in our nervous system too. And sometimes, healing abundance looks like finally believing you can be paid and rested in high favor. It looks like trusting that you don't have to trade your peace for your prosperity.

It looks like allowing in ease.

Becoming a money magnet is not about grinding harder. It's about remembering that your gifts were never meant to deplete you. They were meant to **sustain you.**

I know now that what's meant for me will never be scared away by my worth.

Sometimes that means pausing to say, "Let me get back to you," or taking a moment to calculate everything before responding. Sometimes it looks like workshopping the price with a trusted friend or loved one before sending it off.

With every cake, with every conversation, I get closer to the version of myself who no longer flinches when she says her number out loud.

And until then, I don't mind the flinches. My price is my price.

Every yes I give from alignment is magnetic.
Every boundary I honor calls in abundance.
Every time I trust that I'm worthy of ease, I make space for God to show me just how good it can get.

NOW PLAYING:
♪ *Binz* — Solange

MONEY AND MAGNETISM

Where in my life have I been blocking help or blessings out of fear or control? What does "receiving" look like for me emotionally, spiritually, and financially? When I imagine a life of financial ease, what does my day look like? What stories about money am I ready to release or rewrite?

_____
_____
_____
_____
_____
_____
_____
_____
_____
_____
_____
_____
_____
_____
_____
_____
_____
_____
_____
_____
_____
_____
_____
_____
_____
_____
_____

The Abundant Bank of High Favor
Where Ease Meets Overflow

Add today's date

PAY TO THE
ORDER OF

Add your name or business

$

DOLLARS

Write what you're in need of this season: ex. number of sales, a new salary, a bill paid in full, etc. Add a specific amount if you can.

It's Already Done

Trust that it's already done (because it is!)

GRATITUDE

Take a deep breath and visualize how it will feel when you receive it. *Hold that feeling.* Write 'Thank you' in the space above. After this exercise, continuously revisit that feeling.

"Write the vision and make it plain. If it seems slow in coming, wait patiently, for it will surely take place; it will not be delayed." — Habakkuk 2:2-3 (NLT)

I ALLOW ABUNDANCE TO FLOW INTO MY LIFE FREELY. I AM OPEN TO RECEIVING.

Take a moment to honor the ways abundance and support have already begun moving toward you. Where did you say yes with ease this month? Where did you allow yourself to receive without guilt?

Date:

What I received: (A gift, payment, help, compliment, extra time, peace, etc.)

How it arrived: (Did I ask for it, attract it through alignment, or receive it unexpectedly?)

What came up for me in the moment: (Did I say 'thank you,' and receive it fully, or did I try to downplay or deflect it? Did I feel grateful, awkward, resistant?)

Date:

What I received: (A gift, payment, help, compliment, extra time, peace, etc.)

How it arrived: (Did I ask for it, attract it through alignment, or receive it unexpectedly?)

What came up for me in the moment: (Did I say 'thank you,' and receive it fully, or did I try to downplay or deflect it? Did I feel grateful, awkward, resistant?)

Take a moment to honor the ways abundance and support have already begun moving toward you. Where did you say yes with ease this month? Where did you allow yourself to receive without guilt?

Date:

What I received: (A gift, payment, help, compliment, extra time, peace, etc.)

How it arrived: (Did I ask for it, attract it through alignment, or receive it unexpectedly?)

What came up for me in the moment: (Did I say 'thank you,' and receive it fully, or did I try to downplay or deflect it? Did I feel grateful, awkward, resistant?)

Date:

What I received: (A gift, payment, help, compliment, extra time, peace, etc.)

How it arrived: (Did I ask for it, attract it through alignment, or receive it unexpectedly?)

What came up for me in the moment: (Did I say 'thank you,' and receive it fully, or did I try to downplay or deflect it? Did I feel grateful, awkward, resistant?)

○ New Moon (Menstrual)   Release.
◑ Waxing (Follicular)   Create.
● Full Moon (Ovulation)   Expand.
◐ Waning (Luteal)   Reflect.

Notice when you feel the most magnetic and most confident this month. What days or phases invite you to attract rather than chase?

Menstrual (New Moon) R E L E A S E	*Follicular* (Waxing Moon) C R E A T E

Ovulation (Full Moon) E X P A N D	*Luteal* (Waning Moon) R E F L E C T

If your cycle is irregular, or if you don't have a menstrual cycle at all, try aligning with the moon as a guide. *Remember*: The moon's phases shift every month and won't fall on the same dates, just like the menstrual cycle. Use a menstrual tracker or moon calendar each month to check the dates of each phase before aligning.

INCOME	AMOUNT
TOTAL:	

DEBT	PROGRESS
TOTAL:	

FIXED EXPENSES	ESTIMATE	SPENT
TOTAL:		

VARIABLE EXPENSES	ESTIMATE	SPENT
TOTAL:		

SAVINGS INTENTION	ACTUAL
TOTAL:	

UNEXPECTED BLESSINGS	AMOUNT
TOTAL:	

How can I make it easier to receive? (Compliments, help, payments, opportunities.) Where do I still shrink when it's time to be paid? *Action:* Practice saying "Thank you" without deflecting.

_____

_____

_____

_____

Take a deep breath, relax your shoulders, and notice how abundance showed up for you this month. No judgment. Think of this page as a money journal, not a budget. If this feels overwhelming at any point, pause, take a break, and return when you're ready. *Remember:* awareness is progress.

gentle reminder

Your value is not up
for negotiation.
What's meant for you will never
be scared away by your worth.
You are deserving of overflow.
Money likes you.
Money loves you.
Money is attracted to you.
This is easy.

MONTH FOUR:

PLEASURE AND PLAY

"You can't use up creativity;
the more you use, the more you have."
— Maya Angelou

chapter four.

January 26, 2023

No alarm, so I allow my eyes to open when they're ready. I roll over, stretch, and smile to myself: *I don't have anywhere to be.*

I make a matcha and let the day take me wherever it wants to go. Maybe I'll read for a bit. Maybe I'll ride my bike. Maybe I'll do nothing at all.

The world feels slower when you stop trying to earn your joy.

I go back to Saturday afternoons as a child with my mom and brother. My mom driving, my brother and I in the backseat, a list of errands ahead, but with "All This Love" by DeBarge as our soundtrack, the ride was worth it. So worth it.

The music blasting, the windows down, the three of us singing our hearts out.

After errands, maybe we'd go play tennis, maybe we'd stop for snowballs, or grab a warm Auntie Anne's pretzel. Maybe we'd rush home, excited for the Flintstone Push-

Up Pops waiting for us in the freezer.

Pleasure.
Simple. Easy. *Pleasure.*

I was a curious child, always building, collecting, putting things together.

I can't point to one single thing I loved most; I just remember I loved to create. To learn, to explore, to see something new and say, "Ooo, I want to try that!"

And maybe that's what play really is, following our curiosity.

But along the way, it seems I forgot what that felt like. I got used to waiting for the right time to feel good, for the weekend, for summer, for the next vacation or holiday that gave me permission to rest. I was tired of waiting for joy to be scheduled.

My days started to feel like one long to-do list. Even the things I loved became boxes to check.

It felt like there was this pressure to make everything mean something.

But what if pleasure isn't asking for meaning? What if it just asks for presence?

How could I feel that childlike wonder today?
How could I taste that feeling right now?

During my bike rides, there's a path I love that curves along the river. Riding through the middle of nature, watching the sunlight twinkle through the trees, wind brushing across my face.

Pleasure.

That little girl in me who finds joy in small things, colors, textures, music, and laughter. She shows up when I let my day unfold without control. She shows up when I choose curiosity over obligation.
I feel her returning. I love when I can feel her returning.

In 2021, I started learning how to skate. I was talking to a family friend, Tarsha, about my Aunt Missy's childhood. Aunt Missy is an ancestor I never got to meet, but have always felt deeply connected to. Tarsha and I talked for hours about Missy, about what she was like, her personality, her interests. Tarsha shared that Missy loved skating as a child, every weekend, that's all she wanted to do. After that conversation, my desire to learn how to skate felt like a constant urge, a gentle tug, a love note from Missy.

Sometimes curiosity leads us to connect with our sacred foundation.

Learning to skate, at my big age, was difficult at first. However, it was still something I was determined to learn. Devoted to learn. I fell plenty of times, of course. But even then, it felt like therapy, like something healing me.

Play is freedom in motion.
Pleasure is what happens when we stop trying to earn joy and start creating it.

I used to think pleasure was a luxury.
Now, I know it's a daily devotion.

It's the way I let the day surprise me.
It's the intentional soundtrack as I dance in my living room.
It's noticing the sunset on an afternoon walk.
It's the scent of carrot cake in the oven on a rainy day.
It's the warmth of a long shower that turns into a moment of gratitude.

How can I make *ordinary* pleasure, *mundane* pleasure, my *day-to-day* pleasure?

It's really everywhere.

Now, the practice is intentionally opening my eyes to notice it.

Pleasure and play are not distractions.
Pleasure and play are how *we remember who we are.*

NOW PLAYING:
♪ *Little Things* — India.Arie

PLEASURE AND PLAY

When I was little, what could I do for hours and lose time? What do I love that I'd still do if nobody could see or praise it? Where can I trade "productive" for "play," even for ten minutes? What sounds, textures, colors, scents, or flavors feel delicious to me right now?

_____
_____
_____
_____
_____
_____
_____
_____
_____
_____
_____
_____
_____
_____
_____
_____
_____
_____
_____
_____
_____
_____
_____
_____

I SLOW DOWN ENOUGH TO NOTICE THERE IS BEAUTY EVERYWHERE.

Pleasure Tracker

Where did I allow joy and pleasure to exist in the mundane this month?
List the ways you created or noticed pleasure in your everyday life.
Think about your morning or evening routines. How did you make
them sweeter? What sensations brought you joy? What conversations,
songs, or moments reminded you how good it feels to be *you*?

_____

_____

_____

_____

_____

_____

_____

_____

_____

_____

_____

_____

_____

_____

_____

_____

_____

_____

_____

_____

_____

_____

○ New Moon (Menstrual)   Release.
◐ Waxing (Follicular)   Create.
● Full Moon (Ovulation)   Expand.
◑ Waning (Luteal)   Reflect.

Notice the moments this month when your body felt creative or alive. When was it easy to laugh or create without pressure?

Menstrual (New Moon)
R E L E A S E

Follicular (Waxing Moon)
C R E A T E

Ovulation (Full Moon)
E X P A N D

Luteal (Waning Moon)
R E F L E C T

If your cycle is irregular, or if you don't have a menstrual cycle at all, try aligning with the moon as a guide. *Remember:* The moon's phases shift every month and won't fall on the same dates, just like the menstrual cycle. Use a menstrual tracker or moon calendar each month to check the dates of each phase before aligning.

PLEASURE AND PLAY

INCOME	AMOUNT
TOTAL:	

DEBT	PROGRESS
TOTAL:	

FIXED EXPENSES	ESTIMATE	SPENT
TOTAL:		

VARIABLE EXPENSES	ESTIMATE	SPENT
TOTAL:		

SAVINGS INTENTION	ACTUAL
TOTAL:	

UNEXPECTED BLESSINGS	AMOUNT
TOTAL:	

Where can I increase my income using what I already know or create? *Action*: Write down three ways your skills can make you money this month. Take one inspired step if you desire.

_____

_____

_____

_____

Take a deep breath, relax your shoulders, and notice how abundance showed up for you this month. No judgment. Think of this page as a money journal, not a budget. If this feels overwhelming at any point, pause, take a break, and return when you're ready. *Remember*: awareness is progress.

gentle reminder

Play is freedom.
Pleasure doesn't wait
for the weekend or need permission.
The child in you still knows
how to play, follow your curiosity.

MONTH FIVE:
FAITH AND FLOW

"A lot of people resist transition and therefore never allow themselves to enjoy who they are. Embrace the change, no matter what it is; once you do, you can learn about the new world you're in and take advantage of it."

— Nikki Giovanni

chapter five.

December 31, 2019

The night before I left for New York City, my house was packed.

It was full of my family and friends, who stopped by to send their love. A short prayer after each hug. Everyone saying the same thing: *It'll all work out.*

The next morning, November 18, 2016, I was on my way. My car packed, my heart racing; feelings of certainty, and a hint of fear. I'll never forget the way the clouds looked that day, somewhere between dark and gray, with an ounce of hope that the sun was on its way out.
No job or safety net. All I had was God's voice, first and second month's rent, ambition, and two hundred dollars.

It'll all work out.

Brooklyn was waiting.
I had an interview that same afternoon in Manhattan.
By Tuesday, I had the job. By the following Monday, I was clocking in.

It wasn't quite the dream role, but it was a start.
Faith got me there.

Fast forward to June 30, 2017, the day I quit.
That same morning, Jay-Z released his album *4:44*.
Those angel numbers were a God wink, a reminder: I
am protected, I am aligned, I am okay.

No new job waiting. Once again, only God's voice,
Trust Me. So I did.

Hustle mode: activated.

My dream job had always been to work at SiriusXM.
So while I waited for that yes, I started freelancing.
Saying yes to *everything*.
Hosting events.
Hosting my own internet radio show.

Each yes carried me to the next.

Interviewing celebrities.
BET Awards Red Carpet.
Producing.
Creating.
I was flying!

Then it happened, I received my yes at my dream job.
Lights. Camera. Action!
I did it.

I remember sitting in the studio thinking, *This is it.* This
is the prayer answered. I was doing everything I
wanted to do, everything I once scribbled on post-it
notes and affirmed on my wall was in fruition. Between

being a freelancer, radio host, and producer, I was living my dream.

But even in the middle of my answered prayer, I could feel something shifting. My mornings were spent holding myself together before the day pulled me apart. My train rides to work started to feel like a drag. I'd walk into the studio and feel... off.

This couldn't be it.

I remember thinking, *God, what else? I'm here. Why doesn't this feel like enough?*

I needed it to be enough.

I thought I'd reached the end of the tunnel. That girl who drove from Baltimore to New York City in 2016 could only see this far. *What now, God?*

Months later, it happened again.
I quit.

I was craving more. I needed more. More purpose. More meaning. More fulfillment.
The same faith that led me here was now tugging me forward.

Then, one early Sunday morning in January 2019, God said, "Go home."
Huh!?
Me?

Now?

I didn't understand. I spent the first quarter of 2019 trying to make sense of those instructions. And then, slowly, it started to click.

At first, I thought God meant, "Go home to my city." But God also meant, "Go home to myself."

New York had been my classroom. It taught me courage, trust, and how to move, even when I couldn't see the map. It made me braver. Softer. Louder. Wiser. It turned me into the woman of my dreams, or maybe it just reminded me she was there all along.

So that's what I did. I went home. Summer 2019, I had a farewell party on my rooftop for all my old and newfound friends. The same speech I gave at my farewell party in November 2016: It'll all work out.

But home was a lesson too.
Because when I moved back to Baltimore, I didn't feel finished; I felt undone.

Back in my childhood bedroom, back in the quiet, I kept trying to recreate the same hustle, the same noise. I was chasing the chaos again, chasing the validation of being seen.

Until I realized it wasn't just New York City I was outgrowing, it was the performing.
The proving.

The version of me that needed the world to clap to feel worthy.

That same voice that once told me to go was now teaching me to be.
To write my own stories. To find freedom in the stillness.
To trust that every chapter, even the confusing ones, was flowing me closer to who I'm meant to be.

Every move had purpose. Every detour had direction.
Faith isn't just the leap. It's listening. It's learning that flow is more than forward motion; sometimes it's simply returning.

And, it did all work out.
God's plan wasn't my plan... it was better.

NOW PLAYING:
♪ *Blessings* — Chance The Rapper ft. Ty Dolla $ign

FAITH AND FLOW

Where have I been divinely redirected before, and how did it end up better than I imagined? How can I create peace with where I am right now, instead of focusing on where I think I "should" be?

_____
_____
_____
_____
_____
_____
_____
_____
_____
_____
_____
_____
_____
_____
_____
_____
_____
_____
_____
_____
_____
_____
_____
_____
_____
_____

I TRUST THE DIVINE TIMING OF MY LIFE. EVERYTHING MEANT FOR ME IS RIGHT ON TIME.

This month, explore how it feels to trust that your path is unfolding exactly as it should be. Where are you being invited to let go of control and lean into flow?

Where I'm learning to trust...

Where I'm releasing the need to rush...

This month, explore how it feels to trust that your path is unfolding exactly as it should be. Where are you being invited to let go of control and lean into flow?

Where I'm allowing flow...

How I know I am supported...

○ New Moon (Menstrual)   Release.
◑ Waxing (Follicular)   Create.
● Full Moon (Ovulation)   Expand.
◐ Waning (Luteal)   Reflect.

Notice when you felt resistance this month, and when you felt ease.
What shifted when you stopped forcing and trusted your natural flow
instead?

Menstrual (New Moon)
R E L E A S E

Follicular (Waxing Moon)
C R E A T E

Ovulation (Full Moon)
E X P A N D

Luteal (Waning Moon)
R E F L E C T

If your cycle is irregular, or if you don't have a menstrual cycle at all, try aligning with
the moon as a guide. *Remember*: The moon's phases shift every month and won't fall
on the same dates, just like the menstrual cycle. Use a menstrual tracker or moon
calendar each month to check the dates of each phase before aligning.

INCOME	AMOUNT
TOTAL:	

DEBT	PROGRESS
TOTAL:	

FIXED EXPENSES	ESTIMATE	SPENT
TOTAL:		

VARIABLE EXPENSES	ESTIMATE	SPENT
TOTAL:		

SAVINGS INTENTION	ACTUAL
TOTAL:	

UNEXPECTED BLESSINGS	AMOUNT
TOTAL:	

Do I believe it's safe to have more than enough? *Action*: Replace "I can't afford that" with "How can I make that possible?"

_____

_____

_____

_____

Take a deep breath, relax your shoulders, and notice how abundance showed up for you this month. No judgment. Think of this page as a money journal, not a budget. If this feels overwhelming at any point, pause, take a break, and return when you're ready. *Remember*: awareness is progress.

gentle reminder

You are never behind.
God is always on time.
You can trust what's unfolding,
even when you can't see the full picture.
Every redirection is divine.
What's meant for you
will always find you.

MONTH SIX:
BODY
AND
BLOOMING

"Making peace with your body is your mighty act of revolution. It is your contribution to a changed planet where we might all live unapologetically in the bodies we have."
— Sonya Renee Taylor, *The Body Is Not an Apology: The Power of Radical Self-Love* (2018)

chapter six.

March 16, 2025

*M*oving the coffee table from the middle of the living room to the side every evening was normal. We needed enough space. Donna Richardson, Billy Blanks' Tae Bo, or Shaun T's Hip Hop Abs were the options.

When we weren't moving, there was always a conversation happening.
"No carbs this week."
"Did you weigh yourself today?"
"Don't eat that."

Always about weight. About size. About the "right" way to look. About the "right" way to eat.

And as a child, I absorbed every bit of it.

By the time I reached adulthood, those messages had settled deep into my body.
Move more. Eat less.
I didn't even question them. To me, they were facts.

And somewhere between the squats, jumping all around, and lack of nourishment, I learned that this was what love for your body looked like. Work. *Hard* work.

Even when you didn't feel like it.

The hundred crunches on the living room floor and workout DVDs turned into Shaun T's Insanity and T25, the squat challenge, the plank challenge, and the "no sugar for thirty days" challenge. Then came The Master Cleanse, The Military Diet, The Boiled Egg Diet, and The Cabbage Soup Diet.
Then it became a vegan lifestyle.
Then it became about seeing how long I could stay on the StairMaster.
How many calories could I burn today while eating as little as possible?
Veggie diet.
Fruit diet.
75 Hard.

I spent years swinging between extremes. Every challenge became a test. Each new plan started from the same place: good intention fueled by shame.

I treated my body like a project, not a partner.
I called it "discipline," but really it was fear.
The fear of losing control.
I was terrified of losing control.

When I did hit my goal, I was proud.
So, so proud.

But as soon as the rigidity lifted, so did my results. The moment the challenge ended, the pendulum swung back.

The weight returned, along with exhaustion and disappointment. The voices telling me to try harder next time. The only thing that stayed was the feeling that I had failed again.

I learned early that compliments often came with conditions. That being praised for being smaller felt like approval. That "You look good" usually meant "You look thinner." But wait, not *too* thin. "Are you eating enough?" "I didn't know you ate stuff like that." It took years to unlearn that love isn't measuring you.

I can still remember being on a trip in my twenties, standing in front of a mirror in a two-piece bathing suit. The compliment that came wasn't cruel; it was meant to be kind, but it landed differently.
"Perfection."
And for a moment, I believed it. But later, I couldn't help but wonder, wasn't I perfect before too? Younger me would've loved to hear that.

In April 2022, like clockwork, I was ready to start T25 again. Except this time, I realized I didn't want to do this every day for the next ten weeks. I needed to find new ways to move my body. Ways that felt *good* in this season.

What else did I like to do?
What could I try?

By October 2024, I had explored so many ways

intentional movement could show up in my routine.

I really enjoyed pilates, boxing, and cycling.
I was new to lifting weights, but I loved the way it made me feel.
I tried Solidcore, step aerobics, and dance.
I found joy in walking and jogging.
I even completed my first 5k.

Movement started to look different each day.
It started to become fun.

But movement was just one part of the relearning.
Changing my relationship with food, now *that* was the real test. It was easier to move my body than to feed it with love.

I'd spent so long trying to earn my meals, treating food like a reward or a punishment.
Even after I started moving with intention, I still had to learn how to nourish myself without guilt.

To eat enough to sustain myself. To listen when my body was signaling hunger. She'd been raising her hand, waiting for me to pick her, to love her for years. I was chasing a speedy outcome, without taking my body into consideration.

Was I fueling my body efficiently?

I wanted transformation, but my body was just trying to survive with what I was giving her. How dare I ask her to sustain weight loss too?

A quick Google search confirmed what my body had been saying all along: 1200 calories a day was not nearly enough.
Starvation. Malnutrition. Hormonal disruptions. Digestive issues. Slower metabolism. Fatigue. Trouble sleeping. Anxiety.
These weren't new symptoms; they were my daily reality.

If my body were my best friend, I'd make sure she had a home-cooked meal, made with love. I'd make sure it was filling and nutritious.

I wouldn't treat my best friend like this.

So, I began again.
More listening.
Less judging.

I wanted to be gentle with my body if my weight fluctuated. I wanted to reintroduce balance. I wanted my body to trust itself around our favorite snack. I wanted to enjoy food again.

My body deserved kindness.

So I started showing up differently.
With tenderness.
With patience.

For once, it wasn't about proving how hard I could go. It was about being nourished, eating to live, resting enough, and intentional movement with care.

My current relationship with my body is a product of devotion. I can hold myself accountable without holding myself hostage.

My body is blooming. She's not striving for perfection; *she already is*. In every form she takes. She is mine, and she has carried and protected me through a lot. She is my garden. She tells me when to rest, when to move, and when to reset.

My body is my home, and I'm finally comfortable living here.

NOW PLAYING:
♪ *Masterpiece (Mona Lisa)* — Jazmine Sullivan

BODY AND BLOOMING

What does my body need more of right now? Rest, nourishment, water, sunlight, touch, movement? What forms of movement make me feel alive and connected, not depleted? Can I commit to moving my body as a celebration, not correction? In what ways do I silence my body's signals? How can I begin to honor them again?

_____

_____

_____

_____

_____

_____

_____

_____

_____

_____

_____

_____

_____

_____

_____

_____

_____

_____

_____

_____

_____

_____

_____

_____

_____

Body Positivity Check-In

Take a moment to look at your reflection.
Your body has carried you, protected you,
and evolved with you. Wow! Reconnect with
your body in the present moment.

How has my body shown up for me this year,
even when I didn't notice? In what ways have I
deepened my relationship with my body
since month one? What feels stronger or
wiser within me? What parts of my body
deserve more love, rest, or gratitude?

_____

_____

_____

_____

_____

_____   (add a photo of yourself here)

_____

_____

_____

_____

_____

_____

_____

_____

_____

_____

_____

_____

○ New Moon (Menstrual)   Release.
◑ Waxing (Follicular)   Create.
● Full Moon (Ovulation)   Expand.
◐ Waning (Luteal)   Reflect.

Notice when your body feels most in flow this month. What movements or meals make you feel grounded in your body?

Menstrual (New Moon)
R E L E A S E

Follicular (Waxing Moon)
C R E A T E

Ovulation (Full Moon)
E X P A N D

Luteal (Waning Moon)
R E F L E C T

If your cycle is irregular, or if you don't have a menstrual cycle at all, try aligning with the moon as a guide. *Remember*: The moon's phases shift every month and won't fall on the same dates, just like the menstrual cycle. Use a menstrual tracker or moon calendar each month to check the dates of each phase before aligning.

INCOME	AMOUNT
TOTAL:	

DEBT	PROGRESS
TOTAL:	

FIXED EXPENSES	ESTIMATE	SPENT
TOTAL:		

VARIABLE EXPENSES	ESTIMATE	SPENT
TOTAL:		

SAVINGS INTENTION	ACTUAL
TOTAL:	

UNEXPECTED BLESSINGS	AMOUNT
TOTAL:	

How does my body react when I think about money? Tight? Anxious? Calm? Open? What might that tell me about my relationship with money?

_____

_____

_____

_____

Take a deep breath, relax your shoulders, and notice how abundance showed up for you this month. No judgment. Think of this page as a money journal, not a budget. If this feels overwhelming at any point, pause, take a break, and return when you're ready. *Remember*: awareness is progress.

gentle reminder

Your body desires
connection and partnership with you.
Deep devotion starts with
being kind to yourself.
Your body is on your side,
let it lead.

SISTERHOOD AND CONNECTION

"When we choose to love, we choose to move against fear, against alienation and separation. The choice to love is the choice to connect; to find ourselves in the other."

— bell hooks, *All About Love* (2000)

chapter seven.

March 21, 2021

I regret not fighting for some friendships.

It happened so fast. One day after high school, I looked up, and I didn't have any friends I felt close to. I had plenty of people around me, people I kept in touch with, but I was craving something deeper.

I wanted sisterhood, connection.
I wanted to be seen. I wanted to be known.

I wanted to belong, though I never truly believed I could. I cared about people, I always have, but I didn't know how to be a friend, or at least a good one, and I didn't know how to let anyone be a good friend to me.

For a long time, I didn't trust women. I'd been hurt by them, silenced by them. I learned to brace myself around women. Compliments with side eyes. Jokes that carried half-truths. I had to protect myself.

That meant shielding my heart, guarding my feelings.

Present, but distant.

I'd listen, but rarely share, afraid that my vulnerability would be used against me.

The parts of me I couldn't stand were the same parts I judged in them.

I didn't realize it then, but the first step in finding sisterhood was learning to first love and forgive *myself*. I had to then forgive the women who came before me. Not just the women who came before me, though those wounds shaped me too, it was the culture. The conditioning. The unspoken belief that women couldn't trust each other. "She's acting funny." Friendship was fragile. You had one strike, and you're out.

Imagine if friendships received the same grace as romantic relationships.

Undergrad was the first time I experienced friendship in a way I'd never known before: women who noticed me, considered me, and cared about my inner world. I was learning myself, and they were patient. I came in loud some days and quiet the next, passionate, moody, defensive, on edge, introverted, dysregulated. But nothing was weaponized. I was allowed to be nineteen and human. Our sisterhood held as we all grew, and the gentleness I received became part of who I am today.

Years later, in grad school, I met a woman who felt like divine timing. I was in a new city, miles away from my friends from undergrad. And anytime I entered a new space or environment, I always entered with a shield, preparing for a lonely season, anxious about who I'd talk to or who'd want to talk to me.

In true introverted fashion, I'd usually slip away to my car at lunchtime, counting down the hours until I could go home. One afternoon, she noticed I was gone, and the next day she asked if I wanted to eat with her. That small invitation turned into hours of laughter, and eventually, years of friendship. She taught me what a chosen family looks like, what it means to be seen without having to perform.

But even with the best intentions, sometimes we break what we love because we're scared to say how we feel. I didn't know how to use my voice back then.

When I was hurt, I withdrew.
Instead of talking through it, I shut down.

I didn't give a woman, who meant so much, the chance to understand me. I didn't trust that it would mean anything to her. I didn't trust the connection enough to be honest.

When we stopped speaking, I told myself it didn't matter. People come and go. But it *did* matter, she mattered. I remember being deeply hurt. She was my friend. I wanted to call and tell her about the exciting things that were happening. I wanted to hear about what was going on in her world. We used to talk and laugh for hours on FaceTime. I missed her so much.

I thought about the gentleness and patience I'd been shown all throughout undergrad, and wanted to extend that same grace. I wanted to start over. I wanted to mend that relationship.

Months later, we reconnected. What started as a simple check-in turned into an hours-long conversation: tears, laughter, apologies, grace.

We both named the hurt, but most importantly, we both acknowledged the love, the sisterhood.

I had to unlearn the myths that told me women were competition, and not community. When I became gentle with myself, I learned to become gentle with women too.

Now, I speak up when I'm hurt.
I no longer mind being vulnerable.
I take time to listen.
I let myself be held.

Your evolution doesn't have to come at the expense of sisterhood. Connection *can* navigate time, distance, and new seasons. For me, it's made it stronger.

I regret not fighting for some friendships in my past. But then I'm reminded about the friendships that fought for me.

NOW PLAYING:
♪ *Best Friend* — Brandy

SISTERHOOD AND CONNECTION

When I think of sisterhood, who comes to mind? If no one, let's assess how I feel about nurturing friendships with women: What memories or patterns come to mind? Who might need forgiveness, including myself, to clear space for deeper connection?

_____
_____
_____
_____
_____
_____
_____
_____
_____
_____
_____
_____
_____
_____
_____
_____
_____
_____
_____
_____
_____
_____
_____

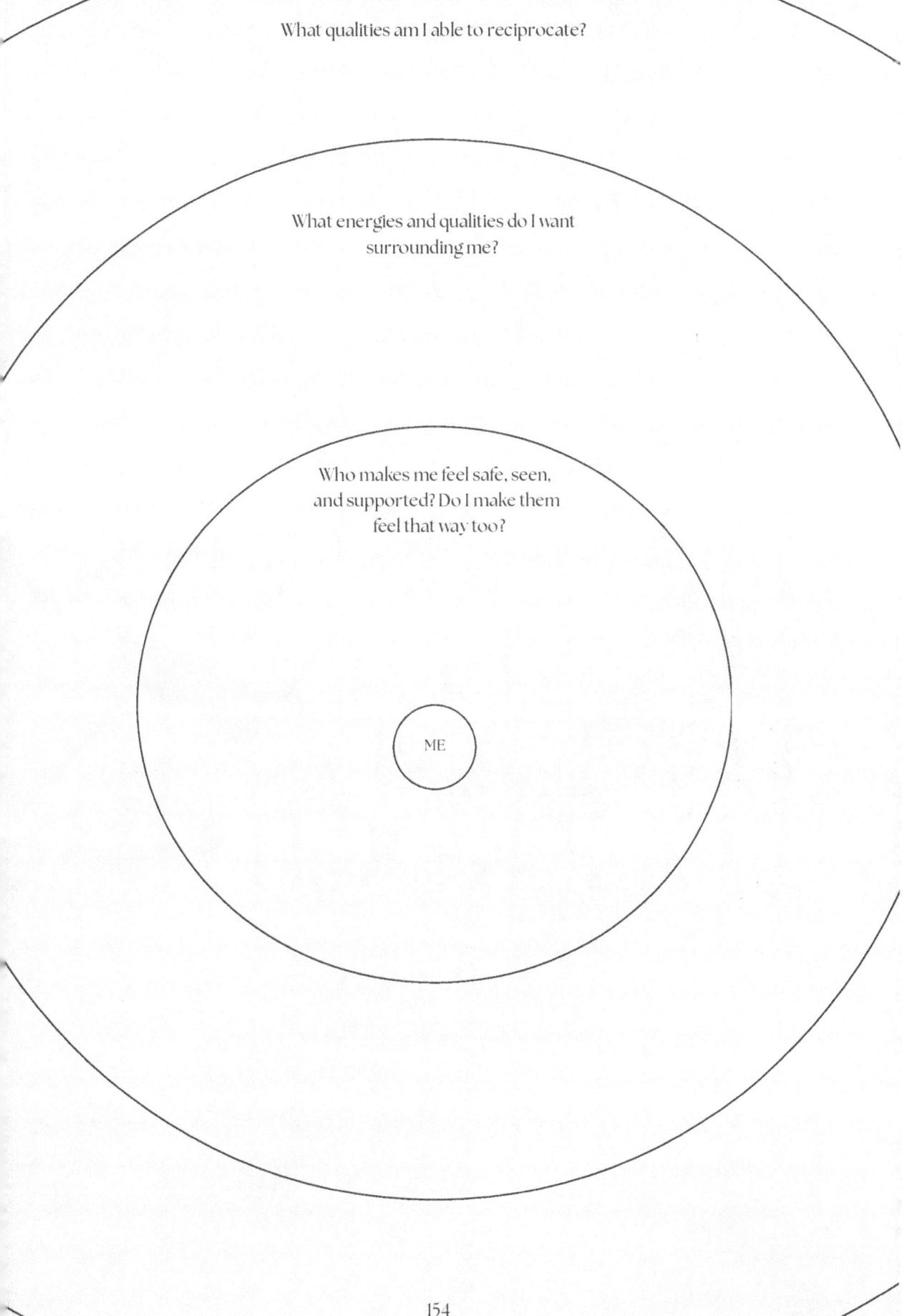

What qualities am I able to reciprocate?

What energies and qualities do I want
surrounding me?

Who makes me feel safe, seen,
and supported? Do I make them
feel that way too?

ME

I ATTRACT RELATIONSHIPS ROOTED IN LOVE AND RECIPROCITY.

Choose one woman (or more) you'd like to reach out to, reconnect with, or nurture your bond with. It could be a friend, a family member, or someone new you feel drawn toward. Ask yourself: What has made this connection meaningful to me in the past? How can I show up with honesty or appreciation? (*Refer back to the traits you are willing to reciprocate*) What simple gesture could I offer: a call, an invitation, or even a compliment or note of gratitude?

If no one comes to mind right now, that's okay. This is an opportunity to reflect and practice self-connection. How can I be the friend I'm longing for? What does being emotionally available to myself look like?

_____

_____

_____

_____

_____

_____

_____

_____

_____

_____

_____

_____

_____

_____

_____

_____

_____

_____

_____

_____

_____

_____

○ New Moon (Menstrual)   Release.
◑ Waxing (Follicular)   Create.
● Full Moon (Ovulation)   Expand.
◐ Waning (Luteal)   Reflect.

Notice when you're longing for connection this month. When do you crave closeness or conversation? When do you pull away and retreat?

Menstrual (New Moon) RELEASE	*Follicular* (Waxing Moon) CREATE

Ovulation (Full Moon) EXPAND	*Luteal* (Waning Moon) REFLECT

If your cycle is irregular, or if you don't have a menstrual cycle at all, try aligning with the moon as a guide. *Remember:* The moon's phases shift every month and won't fall on the same dates, just like the menstrual cycle. Use a menstrual tracker or moon calendar each month to check the dates of each phase before aligning.

INCOME	AMOUNT
TOTAL:	

DEBT	PROGRESS
TOTAL:	

FIXED EXPENSES	ESTIMATE	SPENT
TOTAL:		

VARIABLE EXPENSES	ESTIMATE	SPENT
TOTAL:		

SAVINGS INTENTION	ACTUAL
TOTAL:	

UNEXPECTED BLESSINGS	AMOUNT
TOTAL:	

Who or what could benefit from my financial flow? How can I circulate wealth in alignment with my values? *Action*: Give intentionally this month; to a person, cause, or even your future self (savings account)

_____

_____

_____

_____

Take a deep breath, relax your shoulders, and notice how abundance showed up for you this month. No judgment. Think of this page as a money journal, not a budget. If this feels overwhelming at any point, pause, take a break, and return when you're ready. *Remember*: awareness is progress.

gentle reminder

You are not meant to
go through life alone.
You deserve friendship.
You deserve sisterhood.
You deserve connection.

MONTH EIGHT:
PURPOSE AND PROSPERITY

"Write it down on real paper, with a real pencil, with real intent and watch it get real."
— Erykah Badu

chapter eight.

May 9, 2020

January 26, 2019, I hit "post" on an Instagram photo, sharing my new platform, Chapter Harmony. There was no grand announcement or business plan, simply a vision that felt too big to ignore.

I didn't have all the answers yet, but I knew the time was now. My heart raced, *oh my God! This is it.* My purpose project. I didn't have much time to sit in the moment. I had a 3 p.m. shift at the bar and needed to start getting ready.

That was my life in New York, constant motion, noise. Always rushing somewhere; always chasing the next thing.

It proved to me that hustle *does not* equal purpose. Hustle does not mean fulfillment.

I was doing all the things, working multiple jobs, achieving the goals I thought would make me happy, and yet something in me still wanted more, needed more.

Chapter Harmony would soon teach me that prosperity had nothing to do with hustle and everything to do with *purpose.*

Then came January 2020; by this time, I had been back home in Baltimore for about three months.

And by March, the world slowed down.

No more hustle. No more chaos. No more noise to drown out God's voice. All I had was time.
Time to listen. Time to reflect.
To ask myself who I wanted to be and how I wanted to show up in the world.

In mid-April 2020, the vision for Chapter Harmony's first event came to me, *Harmony & Tea*.
I had two weeks to bring it to life. Two weeks to reach out to my network and plan every detail to perfection. Granted, it was virtual, but everything about Chapter Harmony is an experience. I wanted it to feel like community, like love, like us. I wanted speakers, performers, and music. It had to be a vibe.

April 24, 2020, "Your Event, Harmony & Tea, has been published!" I didn't imagine my first event would be virtual, but something about the network I created in New York and my home base in Baltimore, all able to share space, felt right.

The days leading up to it were full of late nights and early mornings, but not in the same way I was used to; the kind that left me drained. Instead, I was charged, I was alive. Brainstorming and creating had never felt like this before. I couldn't wait to wake up and do it all over again.

Every "yes" from a speaker or performer felt like confirmation.
Every new RSVP felt like alignment.
Fifty available seats.
Sold out.

More women reached out; DMs, emails, messages, asking if there was still room.
Of course, there was.
So, I added fifty *more* seats.
Sold out.

Still. More. Women.
God, this is *crazy*.
I added fifty more.

One hundred and fifty-six seats.
Sold.
Out.

The morning of the event, I woke up calm, passionate, and purposeful. I checked my setup, charged my laptop, and said a prayer. This time, it didn't feel like the dozens of events I'd hosted before.

This felt sacred.

May 9, 2020: The event went live.

The energy.
The community.
The vibe.

Warm.
Soulful.
Sacred.
All created virtually.

Then, the response afterward? *Wow.*
I had never felt anything like it.

And as if God wanted to top it all off, that same
evening, Jill Scott and Erykah Badu blessed us with the
first-ever Verzuz between two women. After an
afternoon of Harmony & Tea, more Neo-soul vibes to
gently rock us to sleep.
Godwink.

My version of success is not defined by how hard I
work. It's defined by how peacefully I sleep at night,
and how eagerly I can jump out of bed to turn around
and pursue it again.

It's by creating peace. Creating love. Creating magic.
Creating community.

It's by allowing God to speak through me.
Moving with intention and allowing prosperity to meet
me there.

Following my curiosity, my fire, my eagerness.

What if this was the purpose all along? Not a destination or an end goal, but just simply feeling something and sharing it so that others can feel it too.

NOW PLAYING:

♪ *Bigger* — Beyoncé

PURPOSE AND PROSPERITY

What genuinely sparks my curiosity, even if I don't know why yet? Where in my life do I feel "lit up" or quietly fulfilled, even in small ways? When do I feel most alive or connected to something bigger than myself?

_____

_____

_____

_____

_____

_____

_____

_____

_____

_____

_____

_____

_____

_____

_____

_____

_____

_____

_____

_____

_____

_____

_____

_____

I AM THE WOMAN OF MY DREAMS. MY PURPOSE UNFOLDS WITH EASE.

My Ideal Day: Living in My Purpose

Use this itinerary template to visualize your dream day from sunrise to sunset if money, time, and fear weren't in the way. Think BIG!

Starting Location:

Morning:
What time did you wake up? What's the first thing you see /do when you open your eyes? How does your body feel? Are you alone or with others?

Midday:
What kind of work, creativity, service, or play is filling your time? What emotions or sensations are you feeling?

My Ideal Day: Living in My Purpose

Use this itinerary template to visualize your dream day from sunrise to sunset if money, time, and fear weren't in the way. Think BIG!

Afternoon
Describe your afternoon. What feels most expansive or rewarding right now?

Evening
Describe your evening. How are you preparing to end the night? What are you most thankful for?

End Location:

Unlock What's Already Yours

Refer back to your itinerary. This version of yourself exists within you right now! How did it feel to live in that energy? What emotions and sensations arose as you moved through your dream day? What moments felt most natural? How can you begin to recreate those same sensations in your life today?

_____
_____
_____
_____
_____
_____
_____
_____
_____
_____
_____
_____
_____
_____
_____
_____
_____
_____
_____
_____
_____
_____
_____
_____
_____

○ New Moon (Menstrual)	Release.
◗ Waxing (Follicular)	Create.
● Full Moon (Ovulation)	Expand.
◖ Waning (Luteal)	Reflect.

Notice when you feel inspired this month and how your environment supports that inspiration. Pay attention to the people and places that seem to align effortlessly when you follow what excites you.

Menstrual (New Moon)
RELEASE

Follicular (Waxing Moon)
CREATE

Ovulation (Full Moon)
EXPAND

Luteal (Waning Moon)
REFLECT

If your cycle is irregular, or if you don't have a menstrual cycle at all, try aligning with the moon as a guide. *Remember*: The moon's phases shift every month and won't fall on the same dates, just like the menstrual cycle. Use a menstrual tracker or moon calendar each month to check the dates of each phase before aligning.

INCOME	AMOUNT
TOTAL:	

DEBT	PROGRESS
TOTAL:	

FIXED EXPENSES	ESTIMATE	SPENT
TOTAL:		

VARIABLE EXPENSES	ESTIMATE	SPENT
TOTAL:		

SAVINGS INTENTION	ACTUAL
TOTAL:	

UNEXPECTED BLESSINGS	AMOUNT
TOTAL:	

How can I align my income streams with my purpose? What feels both profitable and purposeful? *Action*: Research one offer or service that lights you up and could pay you well.

_____

_____

_____

_____

Take a deep breath, relax your shoulders, and notice how abundance showed up for you this month. No judgment. Think of this page as a money journal, not a budget. If this feels overwhelming at any point, pause, take a break, and return when you're ready. *Remember*: awareness is progress.

gentle reminder

Purpose work is
heart work.
Clarity is built through
movement, not perfection.
Hustle chases.
Purpose attracts.
Prosperity responds to purpose.

MONTH NINE:

STILLNESS AND SURRENDER

"In a world that entices us to browse through the lives of others to help us better determine how we feel about ourselves, and to in turn feel the need to be constantly visible, for visibility these days seems to somehow equate to success—do not be afraid to disappear. From it. From us. For a while. And see what comes to you in the silence."
— Michaela Coel

chapter nine.

March 31, 2019

I'm two years old again.
I don't know much yet, but I can tell my parents are separating. No one is saying anything, assuming I wouldn't understand. I'm not sure what I am feeling, but *I can't breathe.*

I'm three years old again, in the backseat of my mom's car, peeking out the window as we pull into our driveway, checking to see if he's there. I used to see my dad every day, but once again, his car isn't in the driveway. Something is changing, but no one's talking to me, assuming I wouldn't understand. I am confused because this feels scary. So, I'll cry. The only way I know how to respond.

I'm fourteen years old again, and today is my first day of high school. This feels really new, and I don't think I like it here because I am way outside of my comfort zone.
My heart is fluttering and unsteady.
The discomfort is too significant to pretend.
I feel overwhelmed.
I feel isolated.
I feel sad.

I'm eighteen years old again, and today is my first day
of college. I'm not sure what led us here, to this big,
unfamiliar city, but this is really far from home.
I don't think I like it; I feel really alone.
It's happening again.

My heart is fluttering and unsteady.
I can't catch my breath.

I. Feel. Sad.

Independence is scary, and I don't want to lose
control. I want to have it all figured out, but what if I
don't have to just *yet*?
What if this is the beginning of something great?
What if everything *will* be okay?

I'm twenty-five years old again.
God, I finally found my rhythm here.
But I think You just told me to leave everything and
move back home.

I'm not sure I understand.
Could You give me the plan first?
My heart is fluttering and unsteady.
I think my body is trying to tell me something.
I feel...

Trust Me.

This time, it doesn't feel as tense.
I'm learning how to regulate my breath.
This feels... *okay*.

Surrender.

I didn't know it was anxiety until I was twenty-four years
old. Emotional, sensitive, fragile, was how people
understood and described me. My body and I, fighting
to understand each other. I thought it was just crying
spells I couldn't explain.

But the day I recognized the patterns was the day I
realized my body had been trying to communicate
with me all along.

Hi, we need something right now.
Hi, we need reassurance.
Hi, we're feeling a bit overstimulated, and a moment to
breathe would be nice.

Relief.

She'd just been trying to protect me all along.
Trying to get me to breathe, *all along*.

Listening meant tuning out the noise and detaching
from my plans. It meant releasing the need for
control. It meant turning inward to reconnect with
God.
To reconnect with myself.

God, what are You saying to me?
Why did You give me this mountain to move?

Though the journey is not linear and twists and turns
are inevitable, every single thing has lined up, even
when I couldn't see how.

In stillness, we find contentment.
In stillness, we're reminded to trust our inner knowing.
In stillness, we must learn to wait.

It's saying, God, I don't know what's next, but I know
You're here.

What if?
But why?
I don't know how...

When I finally stopped fighting the uncertainty, I found
clarity... then peace found me. A feeling I've been
craving all along.

Stillness never promised to erase the fear, but it did
teach me how to breathe through it.

NOW PLAYING:
♪ *When I Wake Up* — Jill Scott

STILLNESS AND SURRENDER

What is something I've been waiting or praying for? That deep desire, I keep asking God, "When is my turn?" How do I show up while I wait? With trust? Impatience? Doubt? Surrender? What might this waiting season be trying to teach or strengthen within me? If I knew I'd receive what I've been waiting for tomorrow, what would I do differently today?

EVERYTHING I WANT, WANTS ME TOO.

A Letter From Me to Me

Imagine it's a year from now. You've received what you were waiting for!
Write a letter from that future version of yourself to the "you" today.
What would they say about this waiting season? What would they thank
you for not giving up on? Gentle reminder: your future self already
knows it all worked out, so let them remind you.

To: My Present self,

_____
_____
_____
_____
_____
_____
_____
_____
_____
_____
_____
_____
_____
_____
_____
_____
_____
_____
_____
_____
_____
_____
_____
_____

Sending you all my love,
From: Your Future Self

○ New Moon (Menstrual)   Release.
◐ Waxing (Follicular)   Create.
● Full Moon (Ovulation)   Expand.
◑ Waning (Luteal)   Reflect.

Notice how your body invites stillness this month. What emotion or need is your body trying to communicate?

Menstrual (New Moon)
R E L E A S E

Follicular (Waxing Moon)
C R E A T E

Ovulation (Full Moon)
E X P A N D

Luteal (Waning Moon)
R E F L E C T

If your cycle is irregular, or if you don't have a menstrual cycle at all, try aligning with the moon as a guide. *Remember*: The moon's phases shift every month and won't fall on the same dates, just like the menstrual cycle. Use a menstrual tracker or moon calendar each month to check the dates of each phase before aligning.

INCOME	AMOUNT
TOTAL:	

DEBT	PROGRESS
TOTAL:	

FIXED EXPENSES	ESTIMATE	SPENT
TOTAL:		

VARIABLE EXPENSES	ESTIMATE	SPENT
TOTAL:		

SAVINGS INTENTION	ACTUAL
TOTAL:	

UNEXPECTED BLESSINGS	AMOUNT
TOTAL:	

What's one financial decision I've been delaying? What clarity can I gain by pausing and planning?

_____

_____

_____

_____

Take a deep breath, relax your shoulders, and notice how abundance showed up for you this month. No judgment. Think of this page as a money journal, not a budget. If this feels overwhelming at any point, pause, take a break, and return when you're ready. _Remember_: awareness is progress.

gentle reminder

Trust the process.
Trust your inner knowing.
Everything is always aligning
and working in your favor.
It's okay to be scared,
just practice breathing through the fear.

PROTECTION AND BOUNDARIES

"I didn't learn to be quiet when I had an opinion.
The reason they knew who I was is because I told them."
— Ursula Burns

chapter ten.

November 18, 2022

As an eldest daughter, I was automatically born alert, born responsible, born nurturing, born protecting.

I was the good girl. The one no one had to worry about. "She'll be fine."

And good meant quiet. It meant agreeable. It meant small. The people pleaser. The people's comfort.

My superpower? Earning love by making things easier for everyone else.

Overextend to overgive,
overgive to overexplain.

I knew what everyone else needed before they asked. I could sense it from a mile away. Not only was I the protector, but I became the fixer, the soother, the adjuster. I'd avoid conflict to avoid rocking the boat.

For heaven's sake, *shh*. Quiet. We need peace. Though the tension in the room was louder than any noise could make.

I used to be afraid to ask for what I wanted.

I never wanted to be too much.
Too direct. Too mean.
I wanted to be easy to love, even if it meant shrinking myself to stay that way.

The scary part about protecting yourself is that you have to be okay with other people's discomfort. I had built my whole life around making other people comfortable, so what happens if they weren't?

Abandonment.
Loneliness.
Loss.

I was hoping that if I made enough sense, if I said it the "right" way, maybe they would understand me, maybe they would stay.

But, a hard pill to swallow: unless it's a mutual exchange, no one owes you anything. Despite all your energy, all your time, everything you gave so willingly.

Despite your love, your sacrifice, and your tireless efforts to keep everything together. Despite it all, they can still choose themselves.

The same feelings of abandonment, loneliness, loss; out of your control.

In May 2022, I let love in.

I had spent the last two years pouring into me, choosing me, so when love showed up this time, I knew it must be right. I didn't interview love. I didn't stop to make sure love had a plan or a purpose. I didn't wonder what love's intentions were for me. I didn't ask for anything from love.
Thank you, God, for my reward for my hard work.
This must be right.

So, I opened my door wide for love to come in.
Into my house. Into my bed.

I made sure love had a place to land. I made sure love had warm sheets and home-cooked meals. I made sure love had clean laundry and proper resources to work. I made sure love had everything it needed; my time, my energy, my all.

I gave and gave and gave to love.
And love took and took and took from me.

As much as I was willing to give, love continued to take.

Love depleted everything I had, but love still needed more.

No worries, love, I will find a way. *And I did.*

I gave more from nothing.

Until one day, I came home ready to greet love, but love was all packed up.

Love was ready to go.

No, no, no. I don't understand. I gave all I had. How could you leave?

I later learned love was not just taking from me, but from anyone else who was willing to give to love.

I've made an error. How could love find a way to show up like this?

God, I thought we did the work? I thought I was healed. We weren't supposed to allow this to happen *again*.

Again, I ask, how could love find a way to show up like this?

I was taught to give. To be generous with my love, my time, my energy. I was devoted to others, without being devoted to myself, and devotion without protection leaves you exposed.

Devotion without protection is *not* love.

How silly of me to give everything to you, without leaving enough for me.
How silly of me to pour from an empty cup, wanting and praying for an ounce back.

How silly of me to leave myself unprotected and still call that love.

Healing in isolation was just the beginning. True healing is revealed in practice, in relationship, when life invites you to apply what you've learned.

I used to think love was measured by our willingness to accommodate.
Now, I believe the depth to which we love others is measured by the depth to which we love ourselves.

Love was just the mirror.
Now, my protection for self runs deeper than relationships.

I desire to show up in my every day protected. To move through this world protected, with intention and discernment.

It looks like trusting my intuition and my body's signals when something feels off. It looks like honoring my need for rest and movement. It looks like being really clear about what I want and what I won't accept.
It looks like saying no to you until I can say yes to me.

There is no external reward for my healing, for pouring into myself and protecting myself.

I am the reward.

No partner, no relationship, no title, no job was ever

meant to be the trophy I placed on my desk for the world to acknowledge, or the medal I wore around my neck for anyone's validation.

The prize was always me.

I deserve to take up space, to change my mind, to say no without guilt. I deserve to speak up and allow honoring how I feel to be reason enough.

I'm a nurturer and a giver by birth; that will never change. But now, anything I give is from overflow.

From protector to protected.
I love you, but I love me first.

NOW PLAYING:
♪ *I Gotta Find Peace of Mind* — Lauryn Hill

PROTECTION AND BOUNDARIES

When do I feel myself tensing or holding my breath throughout the day?
What moments leave me feeling irritated, anxious, or tired, even after
rest? Who do I often feel the need to perform around? Where do I silence
my truth to keep the peace? When do I say yes and instantly regret it?

_____
_____
_____
_____
_____
_____
_____
_____
_____
_____
_____
_____
_____
_____
_____
_____
_____
_____
_____
_____
_____
_____

I CAN BE KIND AND FIRM AT THE SAME TIME. I CHOOSE ENVIRONMENTS AND PEOPLE THAT MAKE ME FEEL SAFE.

SETTING BOUNDARIES

Boundaries sound like...

LET ME THINK ABOUT IT AND GET BACK TO YOU.

I'D LOVE TO HELP BUT MY PLATE IS FULL RIGHT NOW.

LET'S REVISIT THIS NEXT WEEK WHEN I HAVE MORE CAPACITY.

I LOVE YOU BUT I NEED SOME ALONE TIME TO RECHARGE.

I CAN'T MAKE IT THIS TIME, BUT THANK YOU FOR INVITING ME.

THAT TIMELINE DOESN'T WORK FOR ME. HERE'S WHAT'S POSSIBLE.

YOU'RE STANDING TOO CLOSE. COULD YOU PLEASE BACK UP?

NO.

I'D PREFER NOT TO DISCUSS THAT.

I CAN'T TAKE THAT ON, BUT I CAN HELP WITH THIS PART.

I APPRECIATE YOUR PERSPECTIVE, ALTHOUGH I DISAGREE.

THAT MAKES ME UNCOMFORTABLE. PLEASE STOP.

I DON'T ALLOW PEOPLE TO TREAT ME THAT WAY.

I NEED CLARITY ON EXPECTATIONS BEFORE I COMMIT.

I CARE ABOUT YOU, BUT I DO NOT HAVE THE ENERGY TO TALK ABOUT THIS RIGHT NOW.

Set Your Own Boundaries

Boundaries remind us to honor our body's signals. Preparing yourself makes them easier to communicate when the moment arrives. For the scenarios below, you can write your own boundary or use the example provided.

When I feel rushed or pressured to respond, I can say...
ex. "I need time to think about this first."

_____

_____

When I need rest, I can say...
ex. "I need some alone time to recharge. I'll reconnect later."

_____

_____

When I'm asked for more than I can give, I can say...
ex. "I wish I could help, but I'm not in a position to do that right now."

_____

_____

When I feel myself tensing up, I can say...
ex. "I need a moment, let's come back to this later."

_____

_____

When I need clarity before committing, I can say...
ex. "I want to make sure I clearly understand before I say yes."

_____

_____

Are there situations that come up often where having a boundary ready would support you? How can you prepare a boundary for it now?

_____

_____

_____

_____

_____

○ New Moon (Menstrual)	Release.
◑ Waxing (Follicular)	Create.
● Full Moon (Ovulation)	Expand.
◐ Waning (Luteal)	Reflect.

Notice when your body feels protected and safe. What does safety feel like in your body? When does it feel like extra protection is needed?

Menstrual (New Moon)
R E L E A S E

Follicular (Waxing Moon)
C R E A T E

Ovulation (Full Moon)
E X P A N D

Luteal (Waning Moon)
R E F L E C T

If your cycle is irregular, or if you don't have a menstrual cycle at all, try aligning with the moon as a guide. *Remember*: The moon's phases shift every month and won't fall on the same dates, just like the menstrual cycle. Use a menstrual tracker or moon calendar each month to check the dates of each phase before aligning.

INCOME	AMOUNT
TOTAL:	

DEBT	PROGRESS
TOTAL:	

FIXED EXPENSES	ESTIMATE	SPENT
TOTAL:		

VARIABLE EXPENSES	ESTIMATE	SPENT
TOTAL:		

SAVINGS INTENTION	ACTUAL
TOTAL:	

UNEXPECTED BLESSINGS	AMOUNT
TOTAL:	

Where do I overspend? What am I emotionally seeking at that moment? (Comfort, excitement, validation, escape, connection, relief?) What do I actually need instead? (Rest, reassurance, creativity, support, joy, a pause?) How can I meet that need more intentionally to honor both my emotions and my financial peace?

_____

_____

_____

Take a deep breath, relax your shoulders, and notice how abundance showed up for you this month. No judgment. Think of this page as a money journal, not a budget. If this feels overwhelming at any point, pause, take a break, and return when you're ready. *Remember*: awareness is progress.

gentle reminder

You can be kind and firm.
Saying "no" is a
complete sentence.
You do not owe anyone
comfort at the expense of your own.
Your boundaries aren't for
others to understand.
Honoring how you feel is reason enough.

MONTH ELEVEN:

GRATITUDE AND GRACE

"I found God in myself, and I loved her.
I loved her fiercely."
— Ntozake Shange, *For Colored Girls Who Have Considered Suicide /
When the Rainbow is Enuf* (1976)

chapter eleven.

June 13, 2023

*F*orgiveness.

When I think of forgiveness, I think about forgiving myself for holding onto relationships when I knew better, for ignoring the tension in my body and patterns that should have raised red flags.

I think of moments where I should've stayed still, maybe then I could've saved more money. Moments I should've taken more time to think before I acted, to revise before I hit send. I think of moments that I chased when my time could've been used elsewhere.

Grace.

What once made me cringe now makes me chuckle. What once felt like agony now feels like acceptance. What once wanted everything quickly, has learned to trust the timing of my life.

Sometimes life is messy. It can feel like you're moving backward instead of forward. As if time is ticking and one more mistake or delay at this point is just another setback.

I don't have time for this.
I can't afford another deviation from my goal.

But what if that was the whole point? What if that, *too*, is part of the journey?

Forgiveness came to me when I accepted every part of my life: the mistakes, the wrongs, the bad, the ugly.

Forgiveness came to me when I remembered I was doing my best with the tools I had.

Grace met me in the middle of the mess. It greeted me with open arms, ready to rock me like a baby, refusing to let go until I was ready. Grace was remembrance. Remembering my power. Remembering I can choose again. Remembering that at the end of the day, I am still human.

I am reminded of that anxious girl from years ago, who faced her fears and was sometimes knocked down, but never stopped getting back up, again and again, no matter how difficult it was.

Gratitude.

Everything has a purpose, and everything is working together in my favor.

As Tabitha Brown would say, "Oo God, we thank you!" Additionally, Oo God, *I thank me*.

Sometimes we are so close to our present-day that we forget everything that we've gone through; every sleepless night, every tear shed. Everything that led up to this moment.

I am reminded I prayed for this.
I was always living in an answered prayer.

Thank you for not giving up.
Thank you for having that dream, and for having the courage to dream again.
Thank you for wanting more.

What if the joy isn't in reaching the finish line? What if the finish line doesn't even exist? What if there will always be continuous evolution? Something more? More to learn, more to do, more to become? What if the joy is in the little moments along the way?

What if life is about finding God in everything?

I'm grateful for the detours that felt like delays.
I'm grateful for the dreams that ended because they made room for bigger ones.
I'm grateful for the woman I've been, the woman I am, and the woman I'm still becoming.

Freedom.

NOW PLAYING:
♪ *calm & patient* — Jhené Aiko

GRATITUDE AND GRACE

What arrived this year right when I needed it? What prayers have been answered? When did I feel God near? What ordinary moments felt sacred? Where did I offer myself compassion instead of criticism, and what changed because of that gentleness? What loss or delay taught me something I'm grateful for now? What tiny daily ritual reliably brings me back to myself?

_____

_____

_____

_____

_____

_____

_____

_____

_____

_____

_____

_____

_____

_____

_____

_____

_____

_____

_____

_____

_____

_____

_____

GRATITUDE TURNS MY NOW INTO ENOUGH, AND MY ENOUGH INTO OVERFLOW.

Gratitude Jar – Fill Me Up!

Fill this jar however feels good to you. All at once, once a day, or whatever feels right.

I am thankful for...

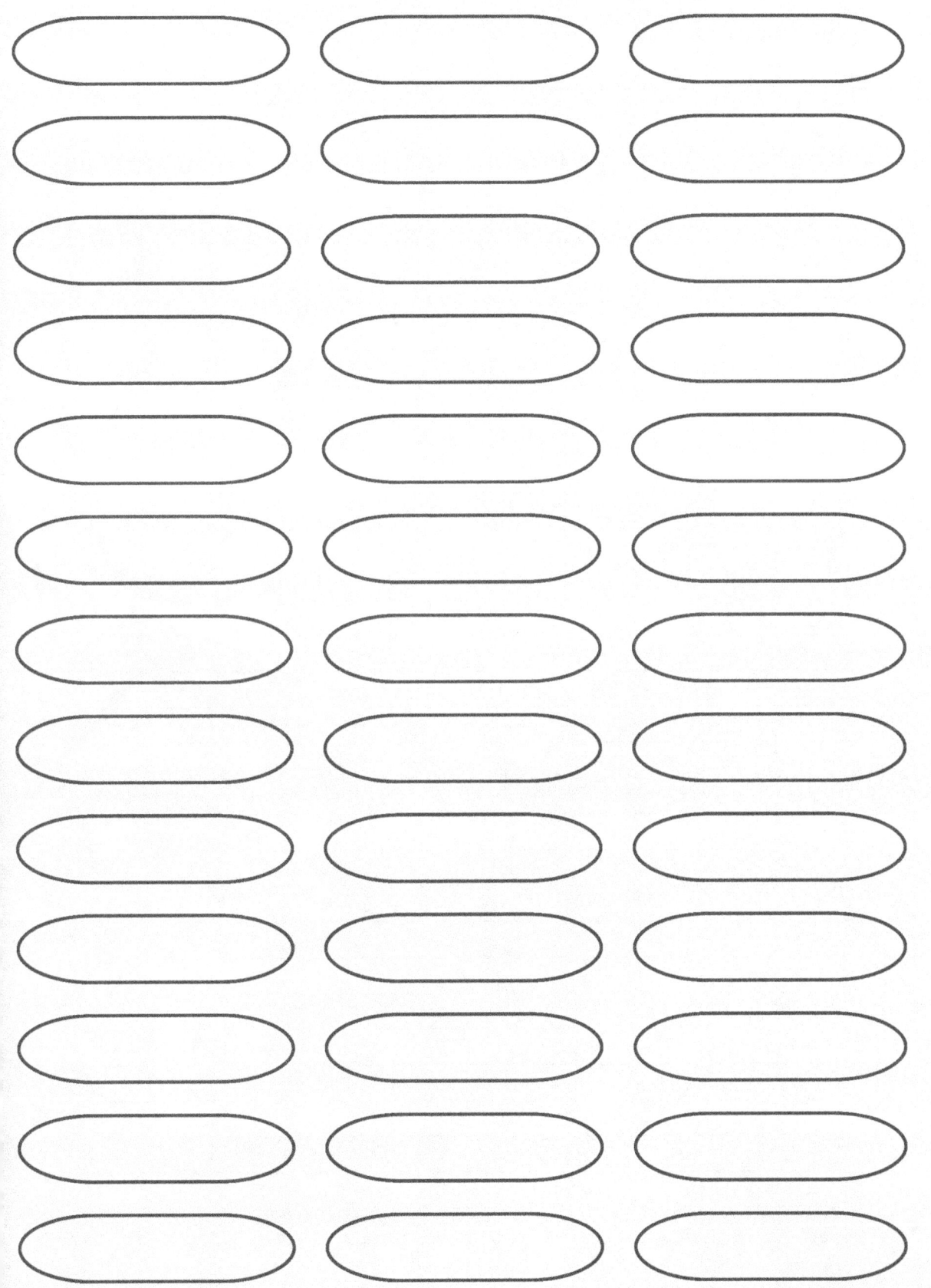

After filling your jar, what themes or blessings showed up most often? Who or what made you feel most thankful this month? What does this list reveal about what truly nourishes you? How can you continue to live from this energy of gratitude daily?

_____
_____
_____
_____
_____
_____
_____
_____
_____
_____
_____
_____
_____
_____
_____
_____
_____
_____
_____
_____
_____
_____
_____
_____
_____
_____
_____
_____
_____
_____
_____

○ New Moon (Menstrual)   Release.
◑ Waxing (Follicular)   Create.
● Full Moon (Ovulation)   Expand.
◐ Waning (Luteal)   Reflect.

Notice what moments invite you to pause and simply say thank you to yourself, your body, and to divine timing.

Menstrual (New Moon)
R E L E A S E

Follicular (Waxing Moon)
C R E A T E

Ovulation (Full Moon)
E X P A N D

Luteal (Waning Moon)
R E F L E C T

If your cycle is irregular, or if you don't have a menstrual cycle at all, try aligning with the moon as a guide. *Remember*: The moon's phases shift every month and won't fall on the same dates, just like the menstrual cycle. Use a menstrual tracker or moon calendar each month to check the dates of each phase before aligning.

INCOME	AMOUNT
TOTAL:	

DEBT	PROGRESS
TOTAL:	

FIXED EXPENSES	ESTIMATE	SPENT
TOTAL:		

VARIABLE EXPENSES	ESTIMATE	SPENT
TOTAL:		

SAVINGS INTENTION	ACTUAL
TOTAL:	

UNEXPECTED BLESSINGS	AMOUNT
TOTAL:	

What am I grateful to have been able to afford, big or small, that made my life feel richer this year?

_____

_____

_____

_____

Take a deep breath, relax your shoulders, and notice how abundance showed up for you this month. No judgment. Think of this page as a money journal, not a budget. If this feels overwhelming at any point, pause, take a break, and return when you're ready. *Remember*: awareness is progress.

gentle reminder

There is always another
opportunity to begin again.
Nothing is wasted;
every moment is your teacher.
The detours, delays, and mistakes
are all working in your favor.
You are living in an answered prayer.

MONTH TWELVE:
HARMONY

"You are your best thing."
— Toni Morrison, *Beloved* (1987)

chapter twelve.

"*It* all worked out!"
"Finally, we reached the light at the end of the tunnel."
"And then they lived happily ever after, *the end!*"

That's how I think of endings.
A clean, resolved finale.

But harmony isn't just an ending, it's also the beginning too.

The integration.
A poetic companion blending the old and the new.

Harmony holds every version of me and every season of my life.

Harmony is balance, pleasure, and well-being. It's alignment. It's the before and the after. It's being in tune with my body, with God, with myself, and letting that connection create purpose.

There was a time when I couldn't hear any of it.
I didn't know what my body was trying to tell me.
I couldn't make out God's voice through the noise.

I didn't know how to reach for inspiration or how to sit still long enough to find it.

Harmony is the inhale and the exhale.
Harmony is the chaos and the deep breath, because I've learned *I needed both.*

I think about the woman, nine years ago, who believed success meant consistency and perfection.

She felt that if she stumbled or paused, people would forget her, that her worth was tied to her productivity.

But when I stopped demanding perfection from myself, I started enjoying the process. I could celebrate the small moments, laugh at my stumbles, and most importantly, learn from them.

I'm not afraid to be seen trying anymore.
I've learned that harmony is not about avoiding failure, but about being brave enough to return to flow, to begin again.
To honor the pauses.
To love the version of me that's in progress, not just the one that's finished.

Harmony is the rest that resets me,
the love that softens me,
the play and the pleasure,
the faith that guides me,
the connections that find me.
Harmony is realizing I was blooming all along.

Harmony is the purpose that anchors me,
the stillness that steadies me,
the boundaries that protect me,
the grace that holds me,
the gratitude that reminds me.

Harmony is the moment I accepted I was whole.

I was always deserving.
I was always enough.

What if life is just a long love letter to self?
The joy, the grief, the lessons, the love; handwritten
and sealed with a kiss. And somewhere in between it
all, we learn that harmony is the space where it all
exists.

My love letter continues: still healing, still growing, still
loving, still building; for the women before me, the girl I
was, the woman I am, and for the children who will one
day know me as home.

Chapter Harmony.

NOW PLAYING:
♪ *Bloom* — Doechii

HARMONY

What lessons or blessings am I carrying into next year that I didn't have before? What part of myself did I rediscover or fall back in love with? What can I release with thanks, knowing it served its purpose? Where in my life do I feel most in harmony right now? Where could I invite more?

_____
_____
_____
_____
_____
_____
_____
_____
_____
_____
_____
_____
_____
_____
_____
_____
_____
_____
_____
_____
_____
_____
_____
_____

I DESERVE TO BE PAID, LOVED, AND RESTED IN HIGH FAVOR.

Take a look in the mirror. Compare the woman you see now to the one you began this journey with. Write a love note to yourself. How have you grown? Emotionally, spiritually, or physically?
What do you radiate now that you didn't before?

_____
_____
_____
_____
_____
_____
_____
_____
_____
_____
_____
_____
_____
_____
_____
_____
_____
_____
_____
_____
_____
_____
_____
_____
_____
_____
_____
_____
_____

○ New Moon (Menstrual)   Release.
◑ Waxing (Follicular)   Create.
● Full Moon (Ovulation)   Expand.
◐ Waning (Luteal)   Reflect.

Notice when thought and movement flow together effortlessly.
What time of day do you feel most aligned?

Menstrual (New Moon)
R E L E A S E

Follicular (Waxing Moon)
C R E A T E

Ovulation (Full Moon)
E X P A N D

Luteal (Waning Moon)
R E F L E C T

If your cycle is irregular, or if you don't have a menstrual cycle at all, try aligning with the moon as a guide. *Remember*: The moon's phases shift every month and won't fall on the same dates, just like the menstrual cycle. Use a menstrual tracker or moon calendar each month to check the dates of each phase before aligning.

INCOME	AMOUNT
TOTAL:	

DEBT	PROGRESS
TOTAL:	

FIXED EXPENSES	ESTIMATE	SPENT
TOTAL:		

VARIABLE EXPENSES	ESTIMATE	SPENT
TOTAL:		

SAVINGS INTENTION	ACTUAL
TOTAL:	

UNEXPECTED BLESSINGS	AMOUNT
TOTAL:	

What worked financially this year? What would I like to do differently next year?

_____

_____

_____

_____

Take a deep breath, relax your shoulders, and notice how abundance showed up for you this month. No judgment.
Think of this page as a money journal, not a budget. If this feels overwhelming at any point, pause,
take a break, and return when you're ready. *Remember*: awareness is progress.

gentle reminder

Don't be afraid
to be seen trying.
Harmony is not a destination.
Harmony holds every version of you.
The joy, the grief, the lessons
and the love are where harmony exists.
You were always deserving.
You were always enough.

Section 3: Sealed in High Favor

YEAR IN REVIEW

This year made me feel...

_____

_____

_____

_____

_____

_____

_____

_____

_____

_____

This year, I became a woman who...
What parts of her did I embody with ease? Where did she surprise me? What qualities did I grow into that I didn't expect?

How did I honor my body and prioritize my rest this year? What routines or practices helped me protect my peace?

What did I learn about receiving? How did I move closer to my business or passion goals? What abundance flowed into my life this year?

How did I love myself differently this year? How did I allow others to love me? What relationships (friendships, family, romantic) deepened or healed?

RYEN'S GOLDEN BUTTER CAKE

THE RECIPE

INGREDIENTS:

VANILLA BUTTER CAKE
- 2 ½ cups all-purpose flour
- 1 ½ cups granulated sugar
- ¼ cup light brown sugar
- 3 teaspoons baking powder
- ½ teaspoon baking soda
- 1 teaspoon salt
- 1 cup unsalted butter, softened (2 sticks)
- ⅓ cup vegetable oil
- 3 large eggs, room temp
- 1 tablespoon pure vanilla extract
- 1 cup whole milk
- ½ cup sour cream

BROWN BUTTER GLAZE
- 4 tablespoons unsalted butter (½ stick)
- 1 cup powdered sugar
- 2 tablespoons whole milk
- ½ teaspoon pure vanilla extract
- Pinch of salt

Standard Bundt pan
Baking spray
Medium saucepan (for browning the butter)
Hand mixer or stand mixer

DIRECTIONS:

- Preheat your oven to 325°F.

- Spray your Bundt pan with baking spray.

- In a large bowl, cream the butter, granulated sugar, and brown sugar. The mixture should be pale and fluffy! Add the eggs one at a time, mixing well until the batter is smooth. Mix in the oil and vanilla, then add the milk and sour cream.

- In a separate bowl, whisk together the flour, baking powder, baking soda, and salt.

- Gently mix the dry ingredients with the wet ingredients. Don't overmix.

- Pour the batter into the sprayed Bundt pan.

- Bake 50-60mins or until a toothpick inserted comes out clean.

- Let cool completely.

- To make your brown butter glaze, melt the butter in a small saucepan over medium heat. As the butter melts, swirl the saucepan occasionally. Once the butter is melted, remove the pan from the heat and let cool for about 2 minutes. In a bowl, mix together: browned butter, powdered sugar, vanilla, salt, and milk. Glaze should be silky!

- Drizzle glaze over cooled cake.

- Serve and enjoy!

I welcome all of life's
pleasures and sweetness.

NOW PLAYING:
♪ *Things I Imagined* — Solange

Thank you for allowing me to share this
space with you.

As you moved through each chapter and each
page, I hope you felt seen, supported, and
celebrated.

I hope this book reminds you that you were always
deserving and you were always enough.

I hope these pages support you in creating more
abundance, more romance, more pleasure, more
rest, and most importantly, more harmony.

You deserve it all.

May each day of your life be proof of how good it
can truly get!

Sending you all my love,
xo, *Ryen*

I am over the moon. Every chapter reminded me that I was writing this book all along.

To my twenty-three-year-old self, my dream girl. I remember going through your journal entries and blog posts, thinking, *"Wow... I know you, but I wish you'd known me."* But it's clear, you were both the dreamer and the dream. Thank you for fighting for me.

All the lessons and breakthroughs were proof that there is purpose in every season, proof that God has never left my side and has always been within me. And for that, I am endlessly grateful.

This book carries the prayers and wisdom of the women who came before me, the women who made me who I am. I am so grateful for my sacred foundation.

To my loved ones and friends, thank you for seeing me. I am so grateful I am surrounded by so much love and support. Lucky me!

To those who held me close, thank you.

Mom, my shotgun rider, your presence was how I first learned to soothe my anxious heart. Thank you for believing in me even when I did not fully believe in myself. I have always been so courageous and eager to jump, even in the midst of anxiousness, because I knew that if I ever fell, you would be there to catch me. That is a luxury I never took for granted. Thank you for being by my side, for listening, for reading my many drafts, and for holding this vision with me. I am so grateful for you.

To my dads separately, I am forever grateful for your love and guidance. Showing up and figuring it out, even without a blueprint, is all I can ask for. Thank you both.

To my siblings, I absolutely adore being your big sister. I am so thankful for your love and comfort. I pray we belly laugh and quote movie and TV lines until the end of time. And Jay, thank you for the way you add even more joy and light to it all. Your humor and encouragement, especially with this project, mean more to me than you know. I am so grateful for you.

Mama and Pop Pop, you've held me close since the very beginning. Thank you for your encouragement, your warmth, and for reminding me to keep sharing my words. I am so grateful for you both.

Alexis, thank you for seeing me, laughing with me, and for being my friend. I am so grateful we get to do life together!

To my sweeties, Dom, Tracy, Ashley, and Aja, thank you for showing me what divine friendship is. Thank you for reminding me that it is possible to learn and grow while in relationship. Thank you for being proof that friends can love you *still.*

Sky, thank you for your gentle reminders to listen to God's voice and to stay on the bike. Your comfort, support, and uplifting words mean the absolute world to me. Thank you.

T, thank you for seeing the vision even before it took shape. Your guidance has been incredibly helpful throughout this process. Forever inspired by you.

To my therapist, thank you for holding my hand as I unravel what it means to heal. For encouraging me to find the words, even when being silent felt easier. For reminding me to feel my feelings, rather than rush past them. I am so grateful for you.

To my editor, Veronica Ojukwu, thank you for your gentle care in refining these pages. I am so grateful for your patience and partnership.

And to every single person who has supported Chapter Harmony since 2019, thank you. Your stories, comments, and messages have fueled this work more than you know. I can't wait to see how this community continues to grow!

Thank you.
Thank you.
Thank you.

Throughout this book, I've added words and songs that have guided and comforted me throughout the years. All rights belong to their respective authors and copyright holders. Their words are included here with love and gratitude for the inspiration their art continues to offer.

"Did you know that birds do not land because they're tired? It is a remembrance. They know and have always known that their liberation depends on their ability to recall the ground." – Cole Arthur Riley, This Here Flesh: Spirituality, Liberation, and the Stories That Make Us (2022)

"Feeling Good" – Nina Simone (I Put a Spell on You, 1965)

"Do you not know that you are the temple of God and that the Spirit of God dwells in you?" – 1 Corinthians 3:16 (NKJV) Scripture taken from the New King James Version®. Copyright © 1982 by Thomas Nelson. Used by permission. All rights reserved.

"God is not a distant creature, far off in the sweet by and by. God is within you. God lives in you, through you, and as you." – Reverend Ike (Frederick Eikerenkoetter II), quote from public sermon and teachings, c. 1970s

"22.22" – Londrelle (Sunflower Soul, 2018)

"In Your Own Home" – Cleo Sol (Gold, 2023)

"As" – Stevie Wonder (Songs in the Key of Life, 1976)

"And so our mothers and grandmothers have, more often than not anonymously, handed on the creative spark, the seed of the flower they themselves never hoped to see; or like a sealed letter they could not plainly read. Guided by my heritage of a love of beauty and a respect for strength—in search of my mother's garden, I found my own." – Alice Walker, In Search of Our Mothers' Gardens: Womanist Prose (1983)

"Private Party" – India.Arie (Testimony: Vol. 1, Life & Relationship, 2006)

"Orange Moon" – Erykah Badu (Mama's Gun, 2000)

"Caring for myself is not self-indulgence; it is self-preservation, and that is an act of political warfare." – Audre Lorde, A Burst of Light (1988)

"Exhale (Shoop Shoop)" – Whitney Houston (Waiting to Exhale Soundtrack, 1995)

"I have the nerve to walk my own way, however hard, in my search for reality, rather than climb upon the rattling wagon of wishful illusions." — Zora Neale Hurston, from a letter to Countee Cullen (1943)

"Find Someone Like You" – Snoh Aalegra (Ugh, Those Feels Again, 2019)

"All successful life is adaptable, opportunistic, tenacious, interconnected, and fecund. Understand this. Use it. Shape God." – Octavia E. Butler, Parable of the Sower (1993)

"This Is for the Lover in You" – Shalamar (Three for Love, 1980)

"Binz" – Solange (When I Get Home, 2019)

"Write the vision and make it plain. If it seems slow in coming, wait patiently, for it will surely take place; it will not be delayed." – Habakkuk 2:2-3, The Holy Bible (NLT) Scripture quotations marked (NLT) are taken from the Holy Bible, New Living Translation, copyright ©1996, 2004, 2015 by Tyndale House Foundation. Used by permission of Tyndale House Publishers, Carol Stream, Illinois 60188. All rights reserved.

"You can't use up creativity; the more you use, the more you have." – Maya Angelou, interview (Bell Telephone Magazine, 1982)

"All This Love" – DeBarge (All This Love, 1982)

"Little Things" – India.Arie (Voyage to India, 2002)

"A lot of people resist transition and therefore never allow themselves to enjoy who they are. Embrace the change, no matter what it is; once you do, you can learn about the new world you're in and take advantage of it." – Nikki Giovanni, American poet and writer

"God Wink" – from When God Winks at You: How God Speaks Directly to You Through the Power of Coincidence by Squire Rushnell (2006)

4:44 – Jay-Z (4:44, 2017)

"Blessings" – Chance the Rapper featuring Ty Dolla $ign, Anderson .Paak, BJ the Chicago Kid, Raury, and Jamila Woods (Coloring Book, 2016)

"Making peace with your body is your mighty act of revolution. It is your contribution to a changed planet where we might all live unapologetically in the bodies we have." – Sonya Renee Taylor, The Body Is Not an Apology: The Power of Radical Self-Love (2018)

"Masterpiece (Mona Lisa)" – Jazmine Sullivan (Reality Show, 2015)

"When we choose to love, we choose to move against fear, against alienation and separation. The choice to love is the choice to connect; to find ourselves in the other." – bell hooks, All About Love (2000)

"Best Friend" – Brandy (Brandy, 1994)

"Write it down on real paper with a real pencil with real intent and watch it get real." – Erykah Badu, via Twitter @fatbellybella (2019)

"Bigger" – Beyoncé (The Lion King: The Gift, 2019)

"In a world that entices us to browse through the lives of others to help us better determine how we feel about ourselves, and to in turn feel the need to be constantly visible, for visibility these days seems to somehow equate to success—do not be afraid to disappear. From it. From us. For a while. And see what comes to you in the silence." – Michaela Coel, Emmy Awards Speech for I May Destroy You (2021)

"When I Wake Up" – Jill Scott (The Light of the Sun, 2011)

"I didn't learn to be quiet when I had an opinion. The reason they knew who I was is because I told them." – Ursula Burns, First Black Woman to serve as CEO of a Fortune 500 Company

"I Gotta Find Peace of Mind" – Lauryn Hill (MTV Unplugged No. 2.0, 2002)

"I found God in myself, and I loved her. I loved her fiercely." – Ntozake Shange, For Colored Girls Who Have Considered Suicide / When the Rainbow Is Enuf (1976)

"calm & patient" – Jhené Aiko (Single, 2023)

"You are your best thing." – Toni Morrison, Beloved (1987)

"Bloom" – Doechii (Alligator Bites Never Heal, 2024)

"Things I Imagined" – Solange (When I Get Home, 2019)

ABOUT THE AUTHOR

Ryen Watkins is a writer, creator, and storyteller devoted to the art of creating intentional pleasure and romance. Through her work and creative platform, *Chapter Harmony*, she invites women to manifest the lives they deserve—to be paid, loved, and rested in high favor.

Stay connected:
@oncloudry
@chapterharmony
chapterharmony.com